Jai Bhim

Jai Bhim

My Judgements in the Light of Ambedkar

Justice K. Chandru

Foreword by Gopalkrishna Gandhi

LeftWord

First published by LeftWord Books, April 2022
Digital print edition, April 2022

LeftWord Books
2254/2A Shadi Khampur
New Ranjit Nagar
New Delhi 110008
INDIA

LeftWord Books and Vaam Prakashan are imprints of
Naya Rasta Publishers Pvt. Ltd.

leftword.com

ISBN 978-93-92018-46-6 (paperback)
978-93-92018-47-3 (e-book)

Visit website

CONTENTS

FOREWORD

Justice Krishnaswami Chandru is a phenomenon.

Are we not, all of us, phenomena?

So we are. Anything born of seed is a physiological phenomenon, anything made of mineral or chemical substance, a material phenomenon. But some of these go on to take their corporeality to a further stage that makes plain phenomena phenomenal. They become something beyond the standard intentions of normal evolutionary processes.

Such phenomenal humans may be found in many branches of life's callings. The law knows of exceptional beings who so integrate the lessons of life with the lessons of law so as to improve both, in equal and mutually enriching measure. This amalgam of life and learning amounts to what I would have called the sixth sense had that phrase – sixth sense – not been already 'booked' to denote an extra-sensory perception, a talent beyond the cognitive powers of the five senses. And so, I will audaciously call this amalgam the seventh sense.

What may that seventh sense be?

I would, with my audacity in speculation continuing, say that persons endowed with the seventh sense are persons who have a distinct capacity, the capacity to be outraged by what their six senses experience. That capacity to be outraged can be creative or destructive. In either case, it is an exceptional sense that makes an ordinary human being a human phenomenon.

For someone steeped in the learning and practice of law, the capacity to feel outraged does something very distinct – it becomes a scalding weapon in the otherwise cold arsenal of reason, logic, codes, procedures, precedents, and dicta. That capacity to feel outraged is not a creation of the law, nor even an adjunct to it. It is a human loan, a gift, a human transference to the profession of law, and being the children of mothers makes us legatees of this inherent sense of order and justice. Somewhat like the capacity to feel, to love, to grieve, is a loan from the house of living to the studios of music or art or sculpture.

Bhimrao Ramji Ambedkar was endowed with that sense of being outraged. He inherited it from life. And he twinned it to his other inheritance, intellectual energy. The two together formed a formidable force, as unbeatable as it was rare. Babasaheb, as he later came to be called by a people who had benefited from that twinning, was a master of the law. He placed his legal training as cold ore is in the furnace of a smeltery, to produce the fiery ingots of a renascent vision, which then became the Constitution of India. He had the seventh sense.

To keep the provisions of that text and the laws that have crowded around it from turning cold again, the world of legal brave-hearts and brave-minds produces for us – thanks be said to our fortune – men and women endowed with that seventh sense. Justice Chandru is a phenomenal example of those. He has alchemized his seventh sense to an alloy that pours its energy into the mould of law, like the molten fluid does in the 'lost wax technique' of panchaloha castings. The result – a rare iconography of justice. His seventh sense is about justice in law, a justice that is un-wearying, un-relenting.

The pages of this slender volume speak of how in India, the land of Ambedkar, the Buddha, Gandhi, Mahavira, Periyar E.V. Ramasamy, and Thiruvalluvar, so much happens in human relationships that must cause outrage but does not. But the pages do so with a distinct message of hope. Outrage and hope? Is that not something of a contradiction? Not so, if we study the achievements of Dr Ambedkar and of his thought-partner, Justice Chandru. The law in India is not a code as much as it is a philosophy of redressal, remedy, and reparation. And, at its best, redemption.

How those oppressed, whether by the stigmata of social mores or the swipes of fortune, can be given a hand by the law, is the story of this volume. We may read it with our own seventh sense awakened – not in despair but in hope.

GOPALKRISHNA GANDHI
CHENNAI

PREFACE

Dr B. R. Ambedkar (1891–1956) was the principal architect of the Indian Constitution. Subsequent to the first general elections of 1952, he also became a member of the central cabinet under Prime Minister Jawaharlal Nehru. Notwithstanding his signal contribution to the framing of the Constitution of India, the government did not confer any honour on him, not in his lifetime nor in the decades after his death. The reason may be that he had quit the first Congress government in protest and also made serious attacks on the foundations of the Hindu religion. It took nearly half a century after his death for the government to confer the highest title of Bharat Ratna on him in 1990. It was only in this year, as the centenary of his birth approached that his portrait was unveiled in the central hall of Parliament.

Notwithstanding the all-around recognition of his services today, the animus against him continues. In 1978, when Marathwada University was sought to be renamed Ambedkar University, it touched off a widespread and violent reaction in Maharashtra, led by the Shiv Sena.

Contrary to this scene, Tamil Nadu showed a different pattern. A revenue district (North Arcot Ambedkar District) and a state-owned transport corporation were named after him in 1979–80. However, with the political consolidation of Other Backward Classes and the emergence of rank communal parties representing them, the different picture presented by Tamil Nadu did not last long. In the late 1990s, severe caste clashes broke out in the southern districts following the establishment of a new transport corporation named after Veeran Sundaralingam, an eighteenth-century warrior from the Pallar community – recognized as a Scheduled Caste. This prompted the chief minister, M. Karunanidhi, to drop caste names from all transport corporations. This was done largely because national leaders had come to be identified with their caste and community. The government declared that henceforth no caste names would be given to districts and withdrew the names of those already named after political leaders.

Amid this overreaction, the name of Ambedkar was also removed, and the district named after him was renamed Vellore, after its headquarters. Fortunately, the T.N. Law University still retains his name. In 2011, litigation relating to the bifurcation of a single metropolitan transport corporation into two corporations, North and South Chennai, came before me. While I upheld the action of the government in bifurcating the corporation due to its unwieldy structure, I also suggested to the government that their action in removing the name of Ambedkar from a transport corporation, due to notions of caste identification, was erroneous and requested them to rename the North Chennai Metro Transport Corporation after Dr Ambedkar. I remarked in my order:

> Before parting with the case, certain observations have to be made for the State to implement. After the bifurcation of Pallavan Transport Corporation Ltd., the Chennai-North Corporation was named after Dr Ambedkar who is the architect of the Indian Constitution. This was the first state to name a transport corporation after a great leader of national status. The whole of India looked with surprise that a state in the southern peninsula of India should name a transport corporation [after] a leader of that stature, something no state had done. Dr Ambedkar does not represent any particular class or caste. His services were not confined to the geographical limit of a particular state. He is one of the tallest leaders of the Indian independence movement. But, in the name of merger of the corporations, his name has been dropped and a general name given to the Metropolitan Transport services.
>
> Though in the case of the other corporations where names

> were dropped, the State might have had its own reasons and an apprehension of law and order problems as well as destruction of public properties, the same yardstick cannot apply in naming the Metropolitan Corporation after Dr Ambedkar. After the formation of North and South Metropolitan Corporations, the Government in G.O.(Ms)No.276, dated 12.10.2010, had stated that for naming of the Corporations, a separate G.O. will be issued.
>
> In the fitness of things, the Government must restore the name of Dr Ambedkar to the Metropolitan Transport Corporation (Chennai-North) Ltd. without any hesitation, and it will go a long way in assuaging the hurt sentiments of many. If the Government can announce such a decision well before 14 April 2011 (i.e., before the birth anniversary of Dr Ambedkar), it will be doing a great service in paying tribute to this tallest of leaders and architect of the Indian Constitution. Even the model code of conduct will not stand in the way as it is only a restoration of the old name given earlier.[1]

The state government did not adhere to my observation. There are thousands of statues of Ambedkar erected in public places throughout the length and breadth of Tamil Nadu, but they have to be protected with iron grills and kept under lock and key; the same is the fate of the Ambedkar statue inside the High Court compound at Chennai. In Cuddalore district, when a statue of Ambedkar located near a roadside was sought to be relocated inside a Dalit colony on the grounds of law-and-order problems, the High Court intervened. Chief Justice Gokhale expressed his concern as follows:

> It is most unfortunate that the statue of Dr B.R. Ambedkar

1 *Metropolitan Transport Corporation Oozhiar Progressive Union vs The Government of Tamil Nadu*, 2011(2) CWC 308. Judgement available on https://indiankanoon.org/doc/1424359/?type=print .

which was already located at a place for more than a year (and which place could not be considered to be in any manner a controversial one), was sought to be shifted to a Dalit settlement. It is highly deplorable that a national leader is sought to be considered as a leader of a community, disregarding his contribution to citizens of India irrespective of their caste, religion, and community.[2]

As a judge of the Madras High Court, I delivered a number of judgments relating to caste and religion, and the writings of Ambedkar undoubtedly came to my help. Unfortunately, many of the judgments were not reported in law journals. Some kind of 'touch me not' attitude persists. Under these circumstances, I decided to publish the gist of my orders and the circumstances under which those cases came before me. Accessible documentation of matters of public importance can draw the attention of young people. This is also why the original publication was in Tamil. Ultimately, the encouragement that I received after its publication gave me the idea of writing in English for a larger audience. Hence this new book.

I thank Gopalkrishna Gandhi for immediately agreeing to write the foreword to my book. I only hope that more than having naming ceremonies and statues to honour Dr Ambedkar, it is his teachings that will be taken to all concerned so that the constitutional vision propounded by him becomes a reality.

2 *T. Amirthalingam vs The State*, 2010 (2) MLJ 1022. Judgement available on https://indiankanoon.org/doc/1083645/ .

1. INTRODUCTION

On 4 March 2014, a day before the schedule for India's general elections was announced, the Manmohan Singh government issued an ordinance[1] extensively amending the Scheduled Castes and Scheduled Tribes (Prevention of Atrocities) Act, 1989. Compelling a Dalit or Adivasi to vote for a particular candidate, or encroaching on land belonging to Dalits and Adivasis, were recognized as caste crimes and brought under the purview of the Atrocities Act. After the elections, however, the Modi government neither amended the law in Parliament nor issued a fresh ordinance to keep the earlier amendment alive – instead, it was allowed to lapse. In 2015, public pressure forced the Modi government to clear another bill in Parliament. The Prevention of Atrocities Act (PoA) now recognized a wide range of offences against Dalits and Adivasis, including economic boycott, words and gestures of a sexual nature, tonsuring of the head and moustache, and abuse using caste-names. The Act also clarifies that a perpetrator's awareness of the victim's identity is to be assumed instead of requiring proof in court. New 'exclusive special courts' would try offences under this Act. They would also ensure completion of the trial within two months from the date of filing the charge sheet. So far, so good.

These amendments did not last long. On 20 March 2018, a bench of the Supreme Court headed by Justice A.K. Goel hearing an appeal case in *Dr Subhash Kashinath Mahajan vs The State Of Maharashtra and Anr.* removed restrictions on granting anticipatory bail to those charged with offences under

1 Scheduled Castes and the Scheduled Tribes (Prevention of Atrocities) Amendment Ordinance. March 4, 2014. Available at https://thc.nic.in/Central%20Governmental%20Ordinances/2014/2014.01.pdf.

the Atrocities Act. Additional 'safeguards' were read into the provisions of the Act. To make things worse, the court also stated its own understanding of the law thus:

> It is necessary to express concern that the working of the Atrocities Act should not result in perpetuating casteism, which can have an adverse impact on the integration of society and Constitutional values.
>
> It has been judicially acknowledged that there are instances of abuse of the Act by vested interests against political opponents in panchayat, municipal or other elections, to settle private civil disputes arising out of property, monetary disputes, employment disputes and seniority disputes.
>
> The liberty of one citizen cannot be placed at the whim of another. The law has to protect the innocent and punish the guilty.
>
> Interpretation of the Atrocities Act should promote the constitutional values of fraternity and integration of society. This may require a check on the false implication of innocent citizens on caste lines.
>
> This Court is not expected to adopt a passive or negative role and remain a bystander or spectator if a violation of rights is observed. It is necessary to fashion new tools and strategies so as to check injustice and violation of fundamental rights.[2]

The judgment sent shockwaves through observers and provoked some strong reactions. Indira Jaising, the well-known senior advocate of the Supreme Court, tweeted:

> Two upper-caste judges of the Supreme Court of India have turned the SC and ST Act from protecting SC/ST to protecting

2 *Dr Subhash Kashinath Mahajan vs State of Maharashtra & Anr.*, reported in (2018) 6 SCC 454). Judgement available on https://indiankanoon.org/doc/108728085/ .

> brahmins, no surprises, the Supreme Court has no SC/ST judges at all.

The Bar Council of India wanted to take action against her.[3] However, the Modi government re-enacted the law the same year, expressing serious objections to the judgment. The 2018 Amendment introduced Section 18A to the PoA Act, which undid the safeguards introduced by Supreme Court in the Subhash Kashinath Mahajan case. The ball was thrown back into the Supreme Court, and petitions challenging the new law were once again before it. With its 2020 decision in the case of *Prathvi Raj Chauhan vs Union Of India* (2020 (4) SCC 727), a full bench of the Supreme Court finally upheld the parliamentary amendment and restored the earlier provisions.

Whatever one may say on the merits of the amendments, the language adopted by Justice Goel is clearly unwelcome. It shows that even officers of the highest judicial order are barely conscious of the discrimination faced by Scheduled Caste and Scheduled Tribe communities, or concerned about improving their access to the machinery of law and order. This is not only true of the Supreme Court; several judges in other courts have expressed regressive views either with their orders or outbursts outside the court.

In an order of 2015, Justice J.B. Pardiwala of the Gujarat High Court made caustic remarks on the reservation issue:

> It is very shameful for any citizen of this country to ask for reservation even after 65 years of independence. When our Constitution was framed, it was understood that reservation would remain for a period of 10 years, but unfortunately, it has continued even after 65 years of independence. Today,

3 'BCI seeks withdrawal of tweet by Indira Jaising.' *The Hindu*, 4 April 2018. https://www.thehindu.com/news/cities/Delhi/bci-seeks-withdrawal-of-tweet-by-indira-jaising/article23430293.ece .

> the biggest threat for the country is corruption. Countrymen should rise and fight against corruption at all levels, rather than shedding blood and indulging in violence for reservation. Reservation has only played the role of an amoeboid monster sowing seeds of discord amongst the people. The importance of merit in any society cannot be understated. Merit stands for a positive goal and, when looked at instrumentally, stands for rewarding those actions that are considered good.

The judge withdrew his remarks and deleted this passage from his judgment hours after 58 Rajya Sabha MPs submitted a motion of impeachment against him for going against the Constitution. Such excesses are not restricted to the higher judiciary. Judges of the lower courts have also exhibited their animus against Dalits and the anti-caste movement.

In 2014, a newly appointed subordinate court judge, S. Devanathan, assumed office in Villupuram district, in northern Tamil Nadu. Finding a picture of B.R. Ambedkar in his court hall (hanging there by custom, along with pictures of Mahatma Gandhi and Thiruvalluvar), he had the picture removed. This infuriated a section of the bar, which went on the warpath. As their complaint against the judge to the High Court was not entertained, the Tindivanam Advocates Association filed a criminal complaint against Devanathan for insulting the architect of the Indian Constitution. But their petition was dismissed with the following observation:

> Respect shown to our great leader is in no way degraded by the act of removal of his portrait, regarding the reason for which two different versions are available, and . . . both the Associations of Tindivanam also [stand] divided. Though the act of removal is likely to hurt the feelings of his followers, the same would not amount to constituting any illegal act, attracting the penal provisions either under SC and ST Act or

> IPC, and . . . does not warrant initiation of any criminal action against the Judge concerned.[4]

Observing a range of insults heaped on leaders from the Dalit community, in December 2015, Parliament had amended the Atrocities Act and inserted a new section 3(1)(t), which identifies as a criminal offence:

> 3(1) Whoever, not being a member of a Scheduled Caste or a Scheduled Tribe, –
> (t)destroys, damages or defiles any object generally known to be held sacred or in high esteem by members of the Scheduled Castes or the Scheduled Tribes
> Explanation: For the purpose of this clause, the expression 'object' means and includes statue, photograph, and portrait.

It is a strange coincidence that the provision was inserted a few weeks after the pronouncement by the Madras High Court. The fundamental question is: should we need parliamentary laws for the holders of high judicial office to respect historical figures and keep constitutional values in mind. The lacuna or shortfall I found was that the system has insulated judges from any outside inputs on the real state of the Scheduled Castes and Scheduled Tribes of this country. For all their schooling and passing through institutions of higher learning, and despite reading the history of constitutional law, they fail to recognize that one-fifth of all Indians are still discriminated against and excluded from equal participation in civil society.

When I decided to start writing on judgments I had rendered relating to caste and religion, I found my understanding enriched by the works of Dr B.R. Ambedkar, which enabled me to navigate

4 *Tindivanam Advocates Association vs The Director General Of Police and Ors*, Crl. O.P. No.13548 of 2014 dt. 27.4.2015. Judgement available on https://indiankanoon.org/doc/8855581/ .

these sensitive and tricky issues. After retiring from the bench in 2013, I decided that these issues should reach a wider section of the people, who for the most part hardly come across or consider the travails of the Scheduled Caste people of this country, and I wrote my book in Tamil. Several good reviews appeared. Across Tamil Nadu, book launch meetings were held. More than ten editions of the book appeared, and the entire income from it was gifted to a school for the underprivileged run by Professor Kalyani, a friend of mine.

At this time, I was asked to head an independent tribunal to go into the question of atrocities against the Scheduled Castes in Tamil Nadu. On 16 August 2014, I conducted an inquiry in Chennai, recording the statements of several Scheduled Caste people and their leaders. My report was later submitted to the state government. The report also came to be published in Tamil and widely circulated. It brought out instances of barbaric indignity heaped on Dalits in Tamil Nadu, a state that boasts of social justice movements going back over a century. Later, I was asked to head the People's Tribunal on Caste Discrimination and Police Action at the University of Hyderabad. This was in the aftermath of Rohith Vemula's death by suicide in January 2016. I conducted the public hearing on 16 April 2016 in Hyderabad and submitted a report to the organizers. Our report brought out the discrimination against Dalits in institutions of higher learning, including central universities. In this context, I decided to bring out my judgments relating to Dalit issues to address wider sections of the public.

As of today, those who most urgently need to be enlightened on the issues dealt with in this book are members of the judiciary, law students and law teachers. They must help make our society more inclusive of the Scheduled Castes and Scheduled Tribes, and everyone needs to work on making the system more just.

2. WHY BUDDHISM?

In his lifetime, Dr B.R. Ambedkar never failed to articulate what he believed to be right. It was his firm belief that the Hindu religion would never ensure economic and social liberty for the Scheduled Castes. This considered belief led him to embrace Buddhism on 14 October 1956, along with three to five lakh followers, at Deeksha Bhoomi in Nagpur.

The next day, Dr Ambedkar himself summed up the story of his conversion and its impact upon him in an address delivered at Nagpur. Speaking in Marathi, he said:

> I started the movement of renouncing the Hindu Religion in 1935 at Nasik and since then I have been continuing the struggle. A mammoth meeting was held at Yeola, in 1935, in which through a resolution a decision was taken to the effect that we should renounce the Hindu religion. In that meeting I had said that though born a Hindu because I could not help it, I would not die as a Hindu. This conversion has given me enormous satisfaction and pleasure unimaginable. I feel as if I have been liberated from hell.[1]

Ambedkar, who shaped the Indian Constitution, incorporated these emancipatory ideas in its preamble:

> JUSTICE, social, economic and political;
> LIBERTY of thought, expression, belief, faith and worship;

1 Massey, James. *Dr B.R. Ambedkar: A Study in Just Society*, Manohar, 2003, p. 39. A roughly similar translation is to be found in *Dr Babasaheb Ambedkar: Writings and Speeches*, Vol. 17, Part 3 (2003), p. 536.

> EQUALITY of status and of opportunity; and to promote among them all
> FRATERNITY assuring the dignity of the individual and the unity (and integrity) of the Nation.

Many believe that Ambedkar borrowed the terms liberty, equality, and fraternity from the philosophy behind the French Revolution. In reality, as he pointed out, he drew these words from his spiritual guru, the Buddha. In a speech of 3 October 1954, given on All India Radio, he revealed this:

> Every man should have a philosophy of life, for everyone must have a standard by which to measure his conduct . . .
>
> Positively, my social philosophy may be said to be enshrined in three words: Liberty, Equality and Fraternity. Let no one, however, say that I have borrowed my philosophy from the French Revolution. I have not. My philosophy has roots in religion and not in political science. I have derived them from the teaching of my Master, the Buddha. In his philosophy, Liberty and Equality had a place only as a safeguard against the breaches of liberty and equality; but he did not believe that the law can be a guarantee for breaches of liberty or equality. He gave the highest place to fraternity as the only real safeguard against the denial of liberty or equality or fraternity which was another name for brotherhood or humanity, which was again another name for religion.[2]

In his Nagpur speech of 15 October 1956, he told his followers why he chose to embrace Buddhism in the following words:

> In fact, this is not something new, nor have we imported it from outside. Buddhism is the religion of this country. It is

2 'The Philosophy My Life', All India Radio speech by Dr Ambedkar October 3, 1954.

> more than two thousand years old. I feel sorry for the fact that I did not embrace this religion earlier. The teachings of the Buddha are eternal but even so, the Buddha did not proclaim them to be infallible. The religion of the Buddha has the capacity to change according to the times, a quality no other religion can claim to have.[3]

A danger awaited the millions who converted to Buddhism. Although the Constitution made reservation benefits available to the Scheduled Castes, these were denied to converts from Hinduism to Buddhism. As per Article 341 of the Constitution, the reservation was applicable to the castes included in the Schedule published by the President of India. Those who converted to Jainism and Sikhism continued to receive reservation benefits. Knowing his conversion call would lead to the loss of benefits, Ambedkar insisted at Nagpur, 'Self-respect is more important than economic gains. Our fight is not merely for economic advancement, but for dignity that we shall gain from self-respect.'

In 1990, the centenary year of Ambedkar's birth, a constitutional amendment was brought in guaranteeing reservation benefits also to those who converted to Buddhism. The Scheduled Caste people who converted to Buddhism were punished for thirty-four years.

For sixteen years after the constitutional amendment came into effect, the Tamil Nadu Public Service Commission continued to practise partiality. In September 2006, an advertisement of the state public service commission appeared in all the leading newspapers – including *The Hindu* – seeking applications to the posts of assistant and personal clerk in the state secretariat service. In matters of direct appointment, the rule of reservation applies to each post separately, but the advertisement asked applicants additionally to consult instructions issued by the state commission.

3 Quoted in *Dr B.R. Ambedkar: A Study in Just Society*, p. 39. Also in *Dr Babasaheb Ambedkar: Writings and Speeches*, Vol. 17, Part 3 (2003), pp. 542–3.

In a note appended to paragraph 11, these instructions stated: 'A member of the Scheduled Castes on conversion to Buddhism will not be entitled to the concession admissible to adi-dravidar Caste (Hindus).' A public-spirited citizen, I. Elangovan, professor of English at Voorhees College in Vellore district, filed a public interest litigation (PIL) against the government, and my decision, in November, quashed the government order. I came down heavily on its brazen disobedience to the Constitution and on the state government's lack of awareness of the reasons why Ambedkar had converted to Buddhism in the first place. I wrote in the judgement:

> The conversion to Buddhism issue did not awake the Government to protect the interests of converted Buddhists and to make available the fruits of reservation. In view of the sustained campaign in different quarters, the Government has thought fit to change their stand on this issue. The idea of doing this came on the birth centenary of Dr Ambedkar, which fell in the year 1990. The central government conferred the highest award of this nation 'Bharat Ratna' posthumously on Dr Ambedkar and unveiled his portrait in the Hall of the Parliament. Apart from this ceremonial exercise, the government thought that a real tribute that may be given to him was to remove the injustice done to the Dalit converts to Buddhism by making a constitutional amendment in the same year. Thus came the constitutional amendment referred to above . . .
>
> It is shocking to note that the state government, and the TNPSC, which is a constitutional creature, have slept over the matter for the last sixteen years and now wake up from their slumber; that too, after a writ petition was filed in the public interest before this Court and to seek this Court's direction, which is not only unnecessary, but such a prayer betrays an abdication of the power vested in them. We have no hesitation

in rejecting the request made by the learned counsel for TNPSC . . .

On the contrary, we issue the following direction to the TNPSC, which is the sole respondent, to remove the note appended in paragraph 11 of the instructions to candidates, which contains the following words, viz. 'A member of the Scheduled Castes on conversion to Buddhism will not be entitled to the concession admissible to adi-dravidar caste (Hindus)' and give a suitable advertisement in all the leading newspapers, in English and in Tamil, with a wide circulation in the State of Tamil Nadu, about correcting the mistake forthwith.[4]

4 *Elangovan vs TNPSC*, rep. by its Secretary, Chennai, 2007(1) MLJ 843 = 2007(2) LLN 2009 (DB). Judgment available on https://www.lawyerservices.in/Elangovan-Versus-Tamil-Nadu-Public-Service-Commission-rep-by-its-Secretary-Chennai-2006-11-23 .

3. RELIGIOUS CONVERSION

Dr Ambedkar's analysis of how caste relates to untouchability can be paraphrased in the following way:

> The root of untouchability lies in the caste system;
> The root of the caste system in varnashrama;
> The root of varnashrama in Brahminism;
> The root of Brahminism is autocracy or political power.

Addressing the Bombay Presidency Mahar Conference in 1936, he had proclaimed that the only way to eradicate untouchability was for the Dalits to leave Hinduism. He observed that the battle between the untouchables and the Hindus would go on forever:

> To put it straight, it can be said that the struggle between Hindus and the Untouchables is a permanent phenomenon. It is eternal, because the religion which has placed you at the lowest level of the society is itself eternal, according to the belief of the high-caste people. No change according to time and circumstances is possible. You are the lowest of the rungs today. You shall remain the lowest forever. This means the struggle between Hindus and Untouchables shall continue forever.[1]

1 Speech delivered by Dr. Ambedkar to the Bombay Presidency Mahar Conference, May 31, 1936, Bombay. Translated from the Marathi by Vasant W. Moon, edited by Frances W. Pritchett. The typescript of the translation, with handwritten emendations, was presented by the translator to Eleanor Zelliot on 25 January 1988, and has been contributed by her for the website: http://www.columbia.edu/itc/mealac/pritchett/00ambedkar/txt_ambedkar_salvation.html .

Further, he advised the Dalits thus:

> From this you will understand one thing: that unless you establish close relations with some other society, unless you join some other religion, you cannot get the strength from outside. It clearly means, you must leave your present religion and assimilate yourselves with some other society.[2]

At the time, M.K. Gandhi was severely opposed to conversion. Heated debates arose on this issue between Ambedkar and Gandhi. I have, on occasion, referred in detail to these issues. The following are extracts from a judgment I delivered in 2007:

> The debate on the question of 'conversion' was not new to this country. Even in the late 1920s, national leaders like Mahatma Gandhi and Dr B.R. Ambedkar debated over this issue. Dr Ambedkar began this discussion by referring to the [first meeting of the 'Federation of] International Fellowship [Conference'] held at Sabarmati in 1928. In this fellowship representatives of different faiths met each other. Mahatma Gandhi was also present at this conference. According to Dr Ambedkar, it was Mahatma Gandhi who raised the issue of conversion in relation to the work of Christian missionaries. After this conference Mahatma Gandhi's opposition to the Christian missionaries' preaching and people getting converted to Christianity is well known. He particularly objected to the spreading of the Christian Gospel among the untouchables. His antagonism to Christian missionaries and the conversion of untouchables to Christianity was based on certain propositions, which according to Dr Ambedkar, were enunciated by him in quite unmistakable terms. Dr Ambedkar selected several propositions to sum up Mahatma

2 Ibid.

Gandhi's position. One such proposition (from the pages of *The Harijan*, 1936) was:

'I do maintain . . . that the vast masses of Harijans and for that matter, of Indian humanity, cannot understand the presentation of Christianity, and that, generally speaking, conversion, wherever it has taken place, has not been a spiritual act in any sense of the term. They are conversions of convenience. They (the Harijans) can no more distinguish between the relative merits (words omitted?) than can a cow. Harijans have no mind, no intelligence, no sense of difference between God and no-God.'[3]

Ambedkar's closing observations in this regard (found on page 450 of the same volume) are as follows:

It is difficult to understand why Mr. Gandhi argues that services rendered by the missionaries are baits or temptations. Why is it not possible to believe that these services by missionaries indicate that service to suffering humanity is for Christians an essential requirement of their religion? . . .

Nobody will deny to Mr. Gandhi the right to save the Untouchables for Hinduism. But in that case he should have frankly told Missions 'stop your work, we want now to save the Untouchables, and ourselves. Give us a chance!' It is a pity that he should not have adopted this honest mode of dealing with the menace of the Missionaries. Whatever anybody may say I have no doubt, all the Untouchables, whether they are converts or not, will argue that Mr. Gandhi has been grossly unjust to Christian Missions . . .

This attitude of Mr. Gandhi's need not deter either the missionaries or the Untouchables. Christianity has come to stay

3 See *Dr Babasaheb Ambedkar: Writings and Speeches*, Vol. 5, Bombay, Education Department, Government of Maharashtra (1990), p. 446.

in India and, unless the Hindus in their zeal for nationalism misuse their political, social, and economic power to suppress it, will live and grow in numbers and influence for good.

How this case came to my court is a strange story, one that shows the continuing struggle between assertions of independence by oppressed communities and the bid to control them from above. In the past, not just common people but rulers too had converted to other religions, transferring state patronage between brahminism, Buddhism, Jainism, Islam, and various Hindu sects. We also have the history of how, once religious leaders had the kings under their control, they persecuted the followers of other religions, as with the execution of Jain munis under the Pandya rule. However, whether the conversions were inspired by the desire for economic gain or for God's grace, they could not destroy the caste system. According to the *Manava Dharmashastra*, better known as the *Manusmriti*, those excluded from the four-varna caste structure were given names such as the *antyaja*, *antyavasayi*, *chandala*, and *shvapaka*. In village society, the outcaste groups came to be marginalized as the *avarna* (no-varna) or *panchama* (fivers, falling outside the four-fold varna order). They were kept away from the village and subjected to social abuse.

The idea that the oppressed castes could escape social abuse by conversion to other religions came to be reinforced by the Christian missionaries in India, especially after the seventeenth century. In the nineteenth century, biblical propaganda and community service by the missionaries brought education to the Scheduled Castes, hitherto denied them. Some could obtain jobs in education, medical services and the army. Despite this, the strong caste system subjected converts to the atrocities of untouchability. These social ills continued to manifest themselves in the form of separate seats in church and separate graveyards.

Incidents of Christian converts returning to the Hindu religion (so-called '*gharvapsi*') also happened in Tamil Nadu. In *Kalam Enum Perunadhi* (2011), S. A. Perumal writes:

> Just as conversion opposed social and cultural oppression, it also opposed economic oppression. This is evident in the history of conversion in Tirunelveli district.
>
> The fisher folk of the seaside village Idindakarai had followed the Catholic religion for nearly 400 years. From the time of colonial rule, an atrocious practice was followed in this village. When the fishermen caught 'Thuvi' fish, they had to give it to the church. Also, half of the total catch on Tuesdays had to go to the church. This was by the order of the Thoothukudi Diocese.
>
> For the poverty-stricken fishermen, this unfair sharing was a big burden. Starting from 1950, there was strong dissatisfaction among the fishermen regarding this practice. They appealed to the head of the church to put an end to this unfair practice.
>
> However, the supporters of the church refused to consider the fishermen's appeal. Consequently, hostility developed between the fishermen and the church and its supporters. In time, this broke out as violent agitation. In the next ten years the hostilities were aggravated by the ex-communication of the fishermen from the church, and police cases were registered against them.
>
> Finding no solution to the problem through violent agitations, the fishermen decided to bring the problem to an end by peaceful methods. They simply decided to reconvert to Hinduism. On 27 October 1967, 843 fishermen converted to Hinduism through Hindu religious rituals arranged by Mysore Saraswathy Swamigal and Kottarasu Arumuga Navalar. Thus, the fishermen, who had been Catholics for 400 years, became Hindus once again and were liberated from the forced sharing of fish with the church.

After this incident, the diocese leaders came to Idindakarai and conducted talks with the fishermen telling them that they need not share their catch with the church and should remain Christians. But the fishermen declined this offer and remained firm about their reconversion to Hinduism.

There were several other sea-side hamlets where the unfair sharing of the fishermen's catch was practised, just as in Idindakarai. But after the Idindakarai reconversion, the church announced that the practice of fish sharing would be discontinued. Thus, the atrocious practice came to an end after the Idindakarai incident.[4]

Ambedkar's experiences had made him realize that just like Hindus, people of other religions too practised untouchability. The Parsis, Christians, and Muslims all ill-treated the Dalits and practised untouchability. Writing on this in Tamil, A. Jaison notes:[5]

> Ambedkar who had believed that only Hindus were possessed by the devil of untouchability, was unable to digest this reality. 'There is no place for untouchability in Islam. Why do they then behave so?' Such questions occurred to him. Ambedkar, at last, realized that the cancer of untouchability, deep-seated in Hinduism, was spreading like a contagious disease to other religions too. 'Through an incident I realized that if a person is untouchable to a Hindu, he is untouchable to a Parsi and also to a Muslim.' How true are Ambedkar's words!

There were, in fact, several instances where Ambedkar came up against the caste venom in India's non-Hindus. *Waiting for a Visa* – written in English, its manuscript was first published in 1990

4 Perumal, S.A., *Kalamenum Perunadhi* (Tamil), Chithirai Publications, Chennai (2011), pp. 112, 113. My translation.

5 Jaison, A., *Sodhanai Theeyil Vilaintha Sadhanai Kathir Ambedkar* (Tamil), Annai Ramabai Ambedkar Publications, 2nd edn (2012), p. 74. My translation.

– recounts how, eleven days into his stay at Baroda as a young man, Ambedkar was driven out of his inn by its Parsi owner and a mob of Parsi men. In that moment of distress, he could not find shelter in the house of an old friend, a Christian, because the friend was married to an orthodox woman who would not have countenanced a Mahar staying with them. Travelling to Aurangabad two decades later, in 1934 – by which time Ambedkar was a public figure who had already founded three newspapers, gained a law degree, two doctorates, and been twice nominated to the Bombay Legislative Council – he and his fellow travellers were accosted by a crowd of angry Muslims and assailed with abuse (such as the pejorative term '*dhed*') for having washed themselves in a tank outside the Daulatabad fort.

However, as the Ambedkar-led mass conversion to Buddhism shows, a change of religions is an important expression of personal and communal protest as well as independence. When free India's Constitution was drafted, people were given the freedom of religious belief. Article 25(1) of the Constitution guarantees this right:

> Freedom of conscience and free profession, practice and propagation of religion –
>
> Subject to public order, morality and health and to the other provisions of this Part, all persons are equally entitled to freedom of conscience and the right freely to profess, practice and propagate religion

After the Constitution came into effect, parties with socially conservative leanings came to power in some states and passed laws that banned religious conversion in their states. In the case of *Rev. Stanislaus vs the State of Madhya Pradesh* (1977), the Supreme Court even passed a verdict validating such a law.[6] After Madhya

6 *Rev. Stanislaus vs State of Madhya Pradesh*, 1977 (1) SCC 677. Judgement available on https://indiankanoon.org/doc/1308071/ .

Pradesh, Arunachal Pradesh, then a union territory, enacted such a law in 1978. In 2000, the newly formed state of Chhattisgarh retained the anti-conversion law of Madhya Pradesh under the title *Chhattisgarh Freedom of Religion Act*, and made it more stringent in 2006. Thus, Article 25 (1) began to be undermined at the state level. Today, such laws exist in Gujarat, Himachal Pradesh, Jharkhand, Odisha, Rajasthan, Uttarakhand, and Uttar Pradesh; another is being framed in Karnataka as this book goes to press.

In 1981, in Meenakshipuram of Tirunelveli District, Tamil Nadu, 1000 persons belonging to 100 Dalit families embraced Islam.[7] S.A. Perumal narrates this incident:

> The Meenakshipuram conversion, which caused quite a sensation all over the country, was a result of social oppression. In April 1980, in Meenakshipuram of Tirunelveli district 1,000 people belonging to 100 Dalit families converted to Islam. This was caused by the oppression of the landed upper caste. For centuries, untouchability was practised there. A majority of Dalits were agricultural coolies. Some few of them were small landowners.
>
> The Dalits were prevented from entering temples. There were separate glasses for them in the tea-shops. They could not use footwear or carry umbrellas. They could not wear clean white shirts. Sexual abuse of Dalit women was rampant. A few educated Dalit youth obtained jobs in cities. In their workplaces there was hardly any oppression of untouchability. So, they wanted to put an end to this evil practice in their native village of Meenakshipuram. They wanted to achieve

7 This is an approximate figure. The count fluctuates due to the weak documentation of the poor, from 1,100 individuals (*India Today*, 15 September 1981) to 600 (*Times of India*, 17 April 2019). The *India Today* report cited above adds that over 2,000 people in Tamil Nadu had changed religions in the first eight months of 1981, compared to less than 1,500 who had done so between 1940 and 1980. The report mentions that anti-Dalit atrocities went up by 80 per cent between 1974 and 1980.

this by a nonviolent method, without shedding blood. In their attempt they encountered the threat of casteist police officials.

The youth held talks with Muslim religious leaders and got converted to Islam. This became sensational news all over India. Towards the end of 1999, the journalist P. Sainath visited Meenakshipuram and conducted a study on the situation 18 years after the religious conversion. 'Now the oppressive evil of untouchability and its humiliation are gone. Equality and self-respect characterize this society.' These were the findings he reported in *The Hindu*.

Following the Meenakshipuram incident, conversion of Dalits to Islam occurred in several other places. These conversions were not motivated by monetary considerations. The aim was to seek self-respect and equality.[8]

Journalist M.P. Udayasooriyan, writing in 2014, quotes Mohamed Haneefa of Meenakshipuram who had converted to Islam:

> I was then 12 years old. We were subjected to severe oppression by the upper castes. In this situation, two upper-caste persons were murdered, and the police hunted down the innocent Dalits, and in the guise of investigation tortured them. To escape the oppression by the upper caste and the torture of the police, we were forced to seek the status of upper caste for ourselves. At once, about 300 families converted to Islam. This became the sensational talk of the nation.
>
> Leaders like Vajpayee and Advani visited our village to hold talks with us. But we stood firm in our conviction that Islam was the only solution for a dignified life. Subsequent to this event several lucky breaks took place in our life. Those who had humiliated us by calling us by our caste names now

8 Perumal, S.A., *Kalamenum Perunadhi*, p. 111. My translation.

> began to address us with the respectful term 'bhai'. The people who had prevented us from walking their streets now invited us to partake of their festival feasts. We embraced Islam and caste divisions against us disappeared. We were accepted as equals, brothers. We are now treated with the respect due to us.[9]

Vali, the Tamil cinema poet, wrote an emotional poem on the creation of Meenakshipuram, which I translate thus:

> The one called Arumugam
> Became Abdullah
> The one called Aiyanar
> Became Antony.
> We showed a different face to them,
> Talked of differences between us
> Thus pushing
> Our brothers away
> And created this.

The religious conversion in Meenakshipuram shocked the nation, particularly Hindus. Many BJP and RSS leaders visited Tamil Nadu in its aftermath. Among the more perverse reactions to this incident was the passage of the Tamil Nadu Prohibition of Forcible Conversion of Religion Act, 2002, a year after J. Jayalalithaa became the chief minister. It stipulated that anyone who wished to convert to another religion had to obtain permission from the district magistrate within a prescribed period. It prohibited conversion for economic considerations – termed as 'allurement'. Human rights activists issued statements condemning the law, saying it took away an individual's fundamental right guaranteed by the Constitution. Catholic priests decided to shut down their

9 Udhayasooriyan, M.P., *Religious Conversion in Meenakshipuram* (Tamil), Puthia Thalaimurai, Flower 5, Petal 24, 6.3.2014. My translation.

educational institutions for one day on 24 October 2002 as a token protest against the law.

Opposing even this token protest, the legal wing of the BJP filed a writ petition in the Madras High Court on 23 October. Four other persons and organizations joined this petition. They persisted with their suit even though the Christian institutions gave an undertaking that no student would be compelled to participate in the protest, and even scheduled an extra day's classes to make up for lost teaching time. The petitioners argued that government-aided institutions, even those with minority status, had no right to protest against the law. In the meantime, faced with opposition from the general public, the law was repealed on 18 June 2004. When the case came up for final hearing in 2007, the anti-conversion law had stood repealed three years already. However, because the petitioner had refused to withdraw the case, it continued to be heard, and our judgment was delivered on 15 March 2007. The judgment compared the school shutdown to protests by lawyers – matters of concern and public inconvenience, but a democratic right nonetheless, which could be exercised responsibly –and concluded that since everyone had the right to protest, the arguments of the petitioner's side were not maintainable. In this context, I recorded Ambedkar's views and opinions on religious conversion in my judgment.[10]

10 *G. Ramanikumar, President, State Legal Cell, Bharathiya Janatha Party, Tamil Nadu &Ors vs State of Tamil Nadu &Ors*, (2007) 6 MLJ 366 = 2007(1) CLT 120). Judgment available on https://indiankanoon.org/doc/138022934/ .

4. PANCHAMI LAND

Contributing to the deliberations of the First Round Table Conference in 1930, Dr Ambedkar and Rettamalai Srinivasan (1860–1945) outlined the terms on which the Depressed Classes would consent to place themselves under majority rule in a self-governing India. This could not happen, they stressed in a joint report, while the Depressed Classes continued in the position of 'hereditary bondsmen. Before majority rule is established their emancipation from the system of untouchability must be an accomplished fact. It must not be left to the will of the majority. The Depressed Classes must be made free citizens entitled to all the rights of citizenship in common with other citizens of the State'.[1]

It is important to note that Ambedkar and Srinivasan expressly rejected the majority community as a determinant of the rights of minorities. (At the Round Table Conference, their joint report formed the appendix to that of the sub-committee on minorities.) Addressing the plenary session of the Conference in November 1930, Ambedkar had also distinguished the Depressed Classes from India's other religious minorities, pointing out that the social and economic status of any single group was quite distinct from its numerical strength. Unlike the Parsis – the smallest religious community in India – whose social and financial standing was comparable to other elite groups, the Depressed Classes were socially persecuted and excluded from access to education, freedom of employment, accommodation, land ownership and public amenities. They occupied a position 'midway between that of a slave and a serf', with the difference that 'the serf and

1 *Dr Babasaheb Ambedkar: Writings and Speeches*, Vol. 2, Govt. of Maharashtra (1982), pp. 503–546.

the slave were permitted to have physical contact, from which the Depressed Classes are debarred'. This injustice resulted from the will of the larger society, and such a society could never be a fair guarantor of their rights. In their report, Ambedkar and Srinivasan also distinguished the Depressed Classes from other labouring sections:

> The helpless, hapless, and sapless condition of the Depressed Classes must be entirely attributed to the dogged and determined opposition of the whole mass of the orthodox population which will not allow the Depressed Classes to have equality of status or equality of treatment. It is not enough to say of their economic condition that they are poverty-stricken or that they are a class of landless labourers, although both these statements are statements of fact. It has to be noted that the poverty of the Depressed Classes is due largely to the social prejudices in consequence of which many an occupation for earning a living is closed to them. This is a fact which differentiates the position of the Depressed Classes from that of the ordinary caste labourer and is often a source of trouble between the two. It has also to be borne in mind that the forms of tyranny and oppression practised against the Depressed Classes are very various and the capacity of the Depressed Classes to protect themselves is extremely limited.[2]

Ambedkar and Srinivasan recommended (in Condition VII) special departmental care for the Depressed Classes. This was not a new idea, for they cited the proceedings of the Board of Revenue of the Government of Madras, almost fifty years earlier. A report (No.723, dated 5 November 1882) sent by the Government of Madras to the British Government had listed various forms of harassment and caste atrocity that were commonplace in the

2 *Dr Babasaheb Ambedkar: Writings and Speeches*, Vol. 2, pp. 552–3.

region, as well as the impossibility for oppressed people to move the courts and have their grievances redressed. Ambedkar and Srinivasan quoted in full paragraphs 134, 135 and 136 of this report:

> 134. There are forms of oppression only hitherto hinted at which must be at least cursorily mentioned. To punish disobedience of Pariahs, their masters:
> (a) Bring false cases in the village court or in the criminal courts.
> (b) Obtain, on application, from Government, waste lands lying all round the 'paracheri',[3] so as to impound the Pariahs' cattle or obstruct the way to their temple.
> (c) Have mirasi[4] names fraudulently entered in the Government account against the paracheri.
> (d) Pull down the huts and destroy the growth in the back-yards.
> (e) Deny occupancy right in immemorial sub-tenancies.
> (f) Forcibly cut the Pariahs' crops, and on being resisted charge them with theft and rioting.
> (g) Under misrepresentations, get them to execute documents by which they are afterwards ruined.
> (h) Cut off the flow of water from their fields.
> (i) Without legal notice, have the property of sub-tenants attached for the landlords' arrears of revenue.
> 135. It will be said there are civil and criminal courts for the redress of any of these injuries. There are the courts indeed; but India does not breed village Hampdens.[5] One must have

3 From '*paraiyarcheri*' or the living areas of paraiyars.

4 Mirasi names and rights were hereditary claims to the ownership or use of land. They were an important component of the colonial revenue system in South India.

5 Literary allusion to Thomas Gray's 'Elegy Written in a Country Churchyard' (1750–51), containing the lines: 'Some village-Hampden that with dauntless breast/ The little tyrant of his fields withstood'. A plucky villager who defends

courage to go to the courts; money to employ legal knowledge, and meet legal expenses; and means to live during the case and the appeals. Further, most cases depend upon the decision of the first court; and these courts are presided over by officials who are sometimes corrupt and who generally, for other reasons, sympathize with the wealthy and landed classes to which they belong.

136. The influence of these classes with the official world can hardly be exaggerated. It is extreme with natives and great even with Europeans. Every office, from the highest to the lowest, is stocked with their representatives, and there is no proposal affecting their interests but they can bring a score of influence to bear upon it in its course from inception to execution.

The conditions cited in 1882 remained recognizable when Ambedkar and Srinivasan cited the report in 1930, and they remain so today. Back in 1891, J.H.A. Tremenheere, the acting collector of Chengalpattu (then Chengleput), had sent a petition to the Government pointing out the pathetic plight of the oppressed classes, and had recommended the sharing of lands with them. His report could melt even a hard heart. As an eyewitness, Tremenheere describes the almost unimaginable poverty of the oppressed:

> [W]ho were covered in dirty rags and were suffering from diseases like leprosy and lived in huts dirtier than a pigsty and from whom the zamindar's men stole even the bottlegourds growing on their thatched roofs.

Tremenheere narrates an incident where villagers prevented a man from the Depressed Class from obtaining *apatta*[6] for the

his rights to the death is likened here to John Hampden, the seventeenth-century parliamentarian who had opposed arbitrary taxation by Charles I.

6 Registry.

poramboke[7] land he had been cultivating for many years because he was a 'pariah'.

Tremenheere also records that the oppressed classes were skilled in taming wasteland and converting it into rich arable land. When they had toiled for many years, converting wooded land, digging wells and cultivating it, the zamindar's men would arrive at harvest time and seize the harvest claiming that these were zamindar's lands[8] and the peasant had no right to cultivate them. Sometimes they would commit atrocities like letting their cattle destroy fields ripe for harvest.

Tremenheere's petition condemned such behaviour of the upper castes.

To counter the atrocities perpetrated on the *Adi Dravidars*, he recommended that these poor people be provided with some land and education. The Government shelved his report. But Christian priests showed interest in the report and arranged for it to be discussed in the British parliament. This resulted in a government order of September 1892, promulgated in the name of Queen Victoria.

As per this order, the Government agreed to distribute among the *Adi Dravidars* lands that had been cultivated by them for years, in order to improve their economic and social conditions. The Revenue Board formed certain rules that would govern such lands:

These lands could not be sold or mortgaged to anyone for ten years after possession.

At the end of ten years, they could be sold or mortgaged only to the Depressed Classes.

Any breach of these conditions would make the assignment liable to be cancelled.

The rules were intended to protect the ownership rights of the oppressed castes and keep the grants from slipping out of

7 Land outside the revenue record, often disused because it is considered inarable or prone to flooding.

8 Grants by the government.

their control. There was provision in the rules for the Revenue Board to confiscate any land that had been illegally transferred. Despite this, the powerful upper castes – and, in the decades after independence, construction companies owned by the dominant castes – took over lands either by force or by using money. Several movements in Tamil Nadu opposed such acquisition of Panchami lands.[9] Revenue officials, waking up to this reality rather late, tried to cancel illegal transactions of Panchami lands in their respective areas. Opposing their attempts, real estate companies approached the High Court.

I decided on one such matter in 2008. A resident welfare association, a private company and others in the Coimbatore district had filed the case in 1996. They sought to prevent the state government from restoring to Dalit ownership lands that had been alienated in this manner. My judgment referred to the history of Panchami lands and found the alienations in clear violation of the rules; hence, I concluded that the revenue officials were entirely within their rights to cancel such illegal transactions. The history I have cited above makes it clear that the State was envisaged as a guardian of not just political but social and economic (distributive) justice. What we call free-market transactions can trend towards coercion, given that some groups enjoy overwhelming control over capital coupled with socio-political dominance. Hence, the State needs to uphold its commitment towards victims of societal bias. I concluded:

> [The] journey into various legal precedents, leaves us with one irresistible conclusion, that the 'Panchami land' assigned in favour of the Dalits as a conditional assignment, if violated, can empower the Government to resume those lands and such

9 The land grants were named after the beneficiaries. Initially called the Depressed Class conditional lands, they began to be referred to in Tamil as '*panchami*', after the *pancham* or 'fivers', i.e., groups left outside the four-fold varna structure of caste society.

> resumed lands can be entrusted to some other beneficiary belonging to the Dalit community. The argument of the present petitioners [is] that they were innocent purchasers, and they did so only on the strength of some letters given by the office of the Sub-Collector or some proceedings of the Board of Revenue in relation to some other issue. In the present case, [where] they were in occupation of the said land and were again willing to buy the land for valuable consideration, [their plea] is stated only to be rejected.

Before ending my judgment, I also took the liberty of quoting a speech by Chief Seattle to the White Army Chief at Washington (quoted earlier by the Supreme Court in one of its judgments).[10] In 1854, the wise Chief Seattle replied to the offer of the great White Chief in Washington to buy their land. His reply was profound. It was beautiful, timeless, and contained the wisdom of the ages:

> How can you buy or sell the sky, the warmth of the land?
> The idea is strange to us.
> If we do not own the freshness of the air and the sparkle of the water,
> how can you buy them?
> Every part of the earth is sacred to my people.
> Every shining pine needle, every sandy shore, every mist in the dark woods,
> every clearing and humming insect is holy in memory and experience of my people.
> The sap which courses through the trees carries the memories of the red man.
> The white man's dead forget the country of their birth
> when they go to walk among the stars.
> Our dead never forget this beautiful earth,

10 *Sachidanand Pandey vs State of W.B.*, reported in (1987) 2 SCC 295. Available on https://indiankanoon.org/doc/497388/ .

for it is the mother of the red man.
We are part of the earth and it is part of us.
The perfumed flowers are our sisters;
the horse, the great eagle, these are our brothers.
The rocky crests, the juices in the meadows,
the body heat of the pony,
and man all belong to the same family . . .

Unfortunately, my judgment was not reported in any of the law journals even though I had laid down certain new principles of law regarding alienation of Dalit-owned lands, viz. that notwithstanding the Transfer of Property Act, the conditional assignment of the land to the Dalits continues and no alienation is permissible. The only consolation is that my judgment was subsequently upheld by a division bench.[11]

11 *VGP Prem Nagar, Minvariya Kudi Erupor Nala Sangam, and others vs The State of T.N.* 2010(6) MLJ337 (DB). Judgement available on https://indiankanoon.org/doc/1890789/ .

5. EQUALITY IN THE BURIAL GROUND

As recently as 2019, a division bench of the Madras High Court had to ask the collector of Vellore why the Dalit community had a separate cremation ground and, further, why they had to struggle to access it. The matter was raised *suo motu* after a news report showed a corpse being lowered on ropes from a bridge into the Dalits' cremation ground. It emerged that they had been denied right of way by two upper-caste Hindus and were compelled to 'air drop' bodies from the bridge to have them cremated. Such stories are not uncommon. In one Tamil Nadu village, the dead bodies of Dalits had to be carried through crop fields because there was no road leading to the Dalit burial ground. When this news was carried in the media, a district collector visited the village and assured the Dalits that measures would be taken to build a separate road leading to their burial ground. Both injustices – separate burial grounds and no road to the one used by Dalits – are commonplace in villages.

The Corporation of Madras, created in 1688, is the oldest municipal corporation of the Commonwealth outside the United Kingdom. In the early twentieth century, the law governing its municipal affairs was amended. The new Madras City Municipal Corporation Act, published on 24 June 1919, stipulated that the corporation would establish and maintain burial/cremation grounds. Subsequent laws passed for the municipalities in districts (1920) stipulated similar duties. However, different communities often had separate sites.

In Thathaneri (Madurai city), there is a huge burial/cremation ground maintained by the Madurai Corporation. Strangely, spaces were allotted here on the basis of caste. The Aryavaisya community in Madurai appealed to the corporation to allot them a separate cremation space. In 2002, the commissioner passed an order to this effect, granting the community a dedicated space of its own for the next five years. The order also stipulated that the permit to the community could not be utilized by another person or any other community. Nearby was a burning shed reserved for the Marwari community. When the Aryavaisyas began to raise a construction at 'their' site, the Marwari neighbours objected. The subject was raised at the corporation council's meeting, and the commissioner revoked his permission to the Aryavaisyas. In 2005, the Aryavaisya community approached the High Court. I heard the case and passed a judgment where I stated that if there was such a rule in the corporation – to provide different spaces for different communities in the burial ground – it contradicted the constitutional guarantee that stipulates equality before law and also Article 17, prohibiting untouchability. I ordered that the communal allocation of spots be cancelled in the burial/cremation grounds maintained by the Corporation and that cremations be conducted only on a first-come-first-served basis:

> Even though the writ petition is dismissed as without merits, it is necessary for this Court to direct the respondent/corporation that the allotment of a separate cremation yard based upon communities or castes should be brought to an end. At least in the departure from this world there can be unity so that apartheid may not be practised by the official acts of the corporation. The corporation must make note of such a direction in future and desist from allotting separate [burning] sheds on a caste basis. The Corporation Act makes it obligatory for the corporation to provide public cremation grounds, but that does not mean that they should be vivisected on the basis of community or caste. While the writ petition is dismissed the Corporation is hereby directed to maintain a

common cremation shed depending upon the requirements in a particular area.

Songs from films have now become people's literature. To drive my point home, I mentioned this and quoted a song from an old Tamil film *Rambaiyin Kaadhal* (1956).

This is the place of equality
Never to be realized in life.
No one is superior
And no one inferior
In this final home of ours.
Where all attain
Peaceful sleep
This is the only place of equality
In this world.
The king sleeps here
So does the pauper
The wise ends up here
And so does the ignoramus.
When they die
They all assemble here
And so
This is the place of equality
Never to be realized in life.

After my judgment, P. Rathinam, a lawyer, filed a public interest litigation that the government be ordered to have burial ground facilities for Dalits. In 2009, this case came up before a division bench headed by Justice P.K. Mishra. The judges who heard the case completely agreed with my judgment and also recalled the film song from it. They mentioned in their judgment:

> In this context, it is unfortunate to notice that even after death, there is some perception regarding segregation. A very illuminating judgment of a learned Single Judge of this Court was brought to our notice while the matter was argued and we are inclined to follow that decision wholeheartedly. As a matter of fact, in the last paragraph of the said judgment, a very touching poem has been extracted, the basic meaning of which is 'in death at least all people are equal'. The laudable object of the said poem should be brought to the notice of each and every individual and no efforts should be made to create a vivisection in the society.

In the same judgment, the judges referred to Article 17 of the Constitution, which prohibits untouchability in any form. They ordered that the Protection of Civil Rights Act, 1955 and the Scheduled Caste and Scheduled Tribes (Prevention of Atrocities) Act, 1989, be strictly implemented.[1] They observed:

> Article 17 of the Constitution of India has the laudable intention of abolishing all forms of untouchability. Article 17 of the Constitution itself declares that enforcement of any disability arising out of 'Untouchability' shall be an offence punishable in accordance with the law. There is no doubt that the protection of the Civil Rights Act has been enacted only with the specific purpose of giving effect to the sentiments in Article 17 of the Constitution of India. In this view of the matter, there cannot be any two opinions about the fact that it is the duty of all concerned and, more particularly, all responsible public officials to ensure that Article 17 of the Constitution is not violated, neither in letter nor in spirit. Similarly, the provisions contained in the Protection of Civil Rights Act and the Scheduled Castes and the Scheduled Tribes (Prevention

1 *P. Rathinam vs State of Tamil Nadu & Others*, 2009(2) CTC 40. Judgement available at https://indiankanoon.org/doc/1585722/ .

of Atrocities) Act, 1989, are required to be enforced strictly. Therefore, it is the duty of such public officials to ensure strict compliance with the provisions of the Constitution as well as the Protection of the Civil Rights Act.

Unfortunately, it is no doubt true that even though over seventy years have elapsed after the passing of the Constitution, the practise of untouchability has not been completely abolished. The need of the hour is to educate the people so that the pernicious practice is abolished sooner rather than later, and all efforts should be made to eradicate any such forbidden practice wherever it raises its ugly head directly or even indirectly.[2]

2 *T. Balasubramanian vs Commissioner, Corporation of Madurai, Madurai,* W.P.(MD) No.3855 of 2005 dated 2.9.2008. Judgment available on https://indiankanoon.org/doc/1898536/ .

6. IMPARTIALITY IN PUBLIC UTILITY SERVICES

Rosa Parks (1913–2005) lived in the state of Alabama, USA. In the city of Montgomery, sixty-six years ago, this African American woman boarded a bus one winter evening on her way home from the tailoring establishment where she worked as a seamstress. She bought her ticket and, as usual, occupied a seat in the 'coloured section'. However, the 'white section' was full, and she was asked to vacate her row of seats so that white passengers standing in the aisle might sit. The three other passengers with her in the row left their seats without demur, but Rosa Parks refused to oblige. She had been a member of the National Association for the Advancement of Coloured People since 1943, and today she got into an argument with the bus crew, asserting her rights. She asked why she should give up her seat when she had bought a ticket and why white passengers should have priority. Her questions were just, but neither the bus crew nor the white passengers wished to speak further with Rosa Parks. The police were called to deal with this troublemaker. They arrested her.

Refusing to accept blatant racism, Rosa Parks did not give up. She canvassed the support of the black population of Montgomery, who rose up to oppose the racist establishment. They took an oath to stop travelling by bus. Instead, they began walking to their workplaces, which dealt a severe blow to the earnings of the municipal bus company – African Americans comprised some 70 per cent of its ridership. Martin Luther King, Jr (1929–1968), who later became a well-known civil rights leader, was an evangelist at the time. He joined the Montgomery protest. As the protesters gained in strength from day to day, spreading out from Montgomery to other cities and eventually the entire country, the system of racial segregation in public areas and amenities came under increased moral pressure, quite apart from the steep decline in income at segregated establishments – whether restaurants, swimming pools or public transport – amid a continuing economic boycott. Three hundred eighty-one days after the protest had begun, on 20 December 1956, the authorities at Montgomery were forced by a court order to end segregated bus seating.

One might ask what the relevance of Rosa Parks' story is here. In India, we have casteism, which is increasingly recognized as analogous to racism. This was the contention of Dalit activists at the World Conference against Racism, Racial Discrimination, Xenophobia and Related Intolerance, held at Durban in 2001. At the time, the activists were widely condemned in India, but the world is growing increasingly aware of the scale of the caste problem and how its practice is akin to racism. In 2013, the European Parliament declared caste discrimination a global evil, laying on its 28 member states the responsibility to combat it. There was a discussion on passing a law equating casteism with racism in the British parliament. In 2018, the Theresa May government caved in to pressure from groups representing upper-caste Hindus and backed out of enacting a law against caste discrimination, but international recognition of the problem continues to grow. Between 2019 and 2021, Brandeis University, Massachusetts; Colby College, Maine; and University of California, Davis, have included caste among the officially recognized forms of discrimination.

Despite being illegal, there is often collusion on the ground between dominant caste groups and the administrative machinery in denying Dalits access to public services. Sivanthipatti is a village 13 kilometres from Tirunelveli in southern Tamil Nadu. There are daily bus services between Tirunelveli and this village. Farmers use the service to transport agricultural produce to the town. Also, students from the village travel to schools and colleges in the Palayamkottai area of Tirunelveli. Entering Sivanthipatti, the buses would first stop at the panchayat board, then at the Amman temple stop, and last at the rice mill stop where a permanent bus shed stood. Alighting at the rice mill stop, people could go to the Dalit colony and the adjoining Kamaraj Nagar.

In 1996, the Sivanthipatti panchayat president was murdered. The story that eventually emerged was that the murder resulted from enmity within the Thevar community – who are classified with the Other Backward Classes but have a dominant position as landowners. In the aftermath, certain elements of the dominant caste indulged in violence against the Pallar community – a Scheduled Caste. Bus services to the village were stopped for a while. Later, when they were resumed, the buses took to stopping near the police station instead of reaching the rice mill terminus. The sudden change greatly inconvenienced the Dalits. Now they had to walk nearly two kilometres to reach their colony. Also, they had to carry their produce on their heads and had to use the streets in which caste Hindus lived, which further complicated their problems. They submitted several petitions to the government-owned Kattabomman Transport Corporation (KTC) officials but to no avail. They were not given any explanation for the change of terminus.

R. Krishnan, a lawyer and social worker, filed a public interest litigation regarding this matter in 1999. Notices were issued to KTC and the police department. But both parties failed to respond. Realizing the seriousness of the matter, the court examined the files and was shocked to find a letter written by Superintendent of Police, Tirunelveli district, to the Government, dated 9 March 2007.[1] It contained the following remarks by him:

> If the bus is allowed to ply upto Kamaraj Nagar, Adi Dravidars of Kamaraj Nagar will occupy the seats fully leaving Thevars

1 Normally, the high court takes 5 to 10 years with final hearing matters. We can only deal with them as and when such matters are listed. It was during the hearing from the government's file that the letter written by the superintendent of police was discovered.

of Sivanthipatti without seat. This will give room for quarrel between two communities once again resulting in breach of peace.

It was found that an IPS (Indian Police Service) officer at the district level had shown caste favouritism in the matter. The court refused to allow this modern form of untouchability. I passed an order for the buses to stop at the rice mill terminus as per the earlier route. Here is an extract of my order from 2007:

> Under the circumstances, it is the bounden duty of the police to educate the local people, by giving wide publicity to the public not to resort to any agitation and give protection to the Corporation to run the buses on the old route, within a period of two weeks from the date of receipt of a copy of this order.
>
> The reasons stated in para 10 of the affidavit[2] amount to violation of Article 21 of the Constitution of India, namely, right to liberty, in not allowing the communities transport to reach their destinations.[3]

2 In the affidavit filed, the Public Interest Petitioner had mentioned that due to the change of bus stop, the Dalits with all their agricultural produce to go to the market will have to walk two kilometres to catch their buses.

3 *R. Krishnan vs Govt. of Tamil Nadu & Others.*, W. P. No. 20298 of 1999 dated 13.3.2007.

7. RESERVATION IN EMPLOYMENT

About the right to reservation in public jobs guaranteed by the Constitution, the Supreme Court observed in 1996:[1]

> The concepts of 'equality before law' and 'equal protection of the laws' guaranteed by Article 14 and its species Articles 15(4) and 16(4) aim at establishing social and economic justice in political democracy to all sections of the society; to eliminate inequalities in status and to provide facilities and opportunities not only amongst individuals but also amongst groups of people belonging to Scheduled Castes (for short 'Dalits'), Scheduled Tribes (for short 'Tribes') and Other Backward Classes of citizens (for short OBCs); to secure adequate means of livelihood and to promote with special care the economic and educational interests of the weaker sections of the people, in particular, Dalits and Tribes so as to protect them from social injustice and all forms of exploitation. By 42nd Constitution (Amendment) Act, secularism and socialism were brought into the Preamble of the Constitution to realize that in a democracy unless all sections of the society are provided facilities and opportunities to participate in political democracy irrespective of caste, religion, and sex, political democracy would not last long.
>
> Dr Ambedkar in his closing speech on the draft Constitution stated on 25 November 1949: What we must do is not 'be content with mere political democracy. We must make our political democracy a social democracy as well. Political

1 Justice K. Ramaswamy in *Mrs Valsamma Paul vs Cochin University and Others*, 1996 (3) SCC 545. Judgement available on https://indiankanoon.org/doc/4735043/ .

democracy cannot last unless there lies at the base of it social democracy . . . Social democracy means a way of life which recognizes liberty, equality, and fraternity as principles of life. They are not separate items but a union of trinity in the sense that to divorce one from the other is to defeat the very purpose of democracy. Without equality, liberty would produce the supremacy of the few over the many. Equality without liberty would kill individual initiative. Without fraternity, liberty and equality could not become a natural course of things.' Articles 15(4) and 16(4), therefore, intend to remove social and economic inequality to make equal opportunities available in reality. Social and economic justice is a right enshrined for the protection of society.

The right to social and economic justice envisaged in the Preamble and elongated in the Fundamental Rights and Directive Principles of the Constitution, in particular, Articles 14, 15, 16, 21, 38, 39 and 46 of the Constitution, is to make the quality of the life of the poor, disadvantaged and disabled citizens of the society, meaningful. Equal protection under Article 14 requires affirmative action for those unequal by providing facilities and opportunities. While Article 15(1) prohibits discrimination on grounds of religion, race, caste, sex, place of birth, Article 15(4) enjoins upon the State, despite the above injunction and the one provided in Article 29(2), to make special provision for the advancement of any socially and educationally backward classes of citizens or for the Dalits and Tribes. Equally, while Article 16(1) guarantees equality of opportunity to all citizens in matters relating to employment or appointment to any office under the State, Article 16(4) enjoins upon the State to make provision for reservation for those sections which in the opinion of the State are not adequately represented in the services under the State. Article 335 of the Constitution mandates that claims of the members of the Dalits and Tribes shall be taken into consideration in

> making appointments to services and posts in connection with affairs of the Union or of a State consistent with the maintenance of efficiency of administration.
>
> Therefore, this Court interpreted that equal protection guaranteed by Articles 14, 15(1) and 16(1) is required to operate consistently with Articles 15(4), 16(4), 38, 39, 46 and 335 of the Constitution, vide per majority in *Indra Sawhney Vs Union of India* [1992] Supp. 3 SCC 217, known as the Mandal case. In other words, equal protection requires affirmative action for those unequals handicapped due to historical facts of untouchability practised for millennia which is abolished by Article 17; for Tribes living away from our national mainstream, [and] due to social and educational backwardness of OBCs.

The system that discriminates against the Dalits is also one of reservations, as it reserves privilege – in the form of education, opportunity, power, and choice – for the oppressor castes. Reservations pervade this system in another sense too, since the reservations – i.e., the inhibitions – of the upper castes determine the degree of freedom available to those lower down. Regarding the role of castes in cooking food, Dr Ambedkar quotes from E.A.H. Blunt's book, *The Caste System of Northern India: With Special Reference to the United Provinces of Agra and Oudh* (1931):[2]

> It is essential to realize that in respect of the cooking taboo, the criterion is the caste of the person who cooks the food, not the caste of the person who offers it. It follows, therefore, that a high caste Hindu can eat the food of a man of any caste, however low, if his host possesses a cook of suitable caste. And that is why so many cooks are brahmins. The Hindu draws a distinction between kachcha food, which is cooked in water and pucca food which is cooked with ghee (clarified butter).

2 *Dr Babasaheb Ambedkar Writings and Speeches* (Vol. 3), Govt. of Maharashtra 1982, p. 105.

> This distinction depends on the principle that ghee, like all the products of the sacred cow, protects from impurity, and since such protection is the object of all food taboos, this convenient fiction enables the Hindu to be less particular in the case of pucca food than of kachcha food, and to relax his restrictions accordingly.

The extract quoted above is part of 'The Hindu Social Order: Its Essential Principles', which Ambedkar had intended as a segment within a book titled *India and Communism*. Its incomplete manuscript was found among his papers after his death.[3]

During the mid-1920s, the caste-based eating arrangements in the Tamil Gurukula School in Cheranmadevi, founded and run by V.V.S. Iyer (1881–1925), caused discord within the Congress Party. Although the Gurukula was a private institution, the Congress had financed it. Leaders like E.V. Ramasamy (Periyar) and Dr P. Varadarajulu Naidu were united in their opposition to the eating arrangements practised at the Gurukula – where it emerged that two brahmin boys were being fed in a separate room from the other students. Dr Naidu and EVR were instrumental in getting a majority resolution passed, which said that the financial support extended by the Congress Committee would be withdrawn if the Gurukula management did not stop this casteist practice.

In the midst of this controversy and in reply to a letter from Dr Naidu, Mahatma Gandhi wrote to him on 10 March 1925:[4]

> With reference to the Gurukul controversy I told Mr. Iyer that I would not give a definite opinion unless I had seen you and heard you. Having heard you, it seems to me that in so far as the present brahmacharis are concerned, if the parents of the brahmin boys insist on their boys being allowed to dine

3 B. R. Ambedkar, *India and Communism*, introduction by Anand Teltumbde, New Delhi: LeftWord Books, 2017.

4 *Collected Works of Mahatma Gandhi*, Vol. 30, p. 371.

> separately, their scruples should be respected. But, for the future, it may be announced that no brahmacharis would be accepted whose parents would not let their boys dine in the same row with the others. I understand from you that the cook at the Gurukul would be always a brahmin. What you object to (and that properly) is the separating of non-brahmin boys from the brahmins. I do think that all the boys should sit in the same row whilst they are taking their meals.

Although the Congress had passed a resolution giving an ultimatum to the Gurukula, opinions within the Congress Committee of Tamil Nadu remained divided in this matter, and EVR and Varadharajulu Naidu resigned from the Congress. Later, to eradicate caste divisions in society, several *samapandhi* feasts – or inter-caste dining events – were arranged by political leaders as a social measure.

When K. Kamaraj was chief minister of Tamil Nadu (1954–63), noon meals began to be provided in some schools on a trial basis. The wheat bran, soya, oil, and milk powder supplied by the U.S. Government under the P.L. 480 scheme was used for this. It was not run as a comprehensive scheme. Moreover, in the face of strong opposition from developing countries whose agriculture was being wrecked by the heavily subsidized US farm sector exports, the United States revised its food aid programme in 1966. Thereafter, when M.G. Ramachandran was chief minister (1977–87), he introduced a noon meal scheme in all schools. Introduced with financial assistance to village panchayats, the entire scheme was later brought under the control of the Social Welfare Department.

With Tamil Nadu's success in implementing the scheme, a national launch was envisioned in 1995. However, state governments did not implement it till the Supreme Court intervened in November 2001 with an order that primary schools across the country start providing mid-day meals for at least 200 days in the year, even specifying their minimum calorific value (300 calories) and protein component (8–12 grams).

Following M.G. Ramachandran's initiative, noon meal centres were established across Tamil Nadu in every school run or aided by the government or city corporation. Three posts were created at each centre – those of noon meal organizer, cook, and assistant. A government order of 1997 imposed the condition that any women selected for these posts should live within 1 km of the village where the centre was located. While nearly one lakh posts were created in noon meal centres throughout Tamil Nadu, no reservation was made for women belonging to the Scheduled Castes. Moreover, because of the 1 km rule, Dalit women were disqualified from applying for the post. Since the Dalit neighbourhoods were outside the village limits, these women were automatically excluded from appointments. This iniquity occurred despite the fact that selection to these posts was made by the state government or under its direct supervision, and the centres were funded entirely by the central government, i.e., with public money. Reservation was not provided for SC and ST employees. Such 'oversights' have a convenient tendency of working to the detriment of disadvantaged groups. In the appointments of workers to Anganwadi Centres or crèches, the government acted with the same partiality. Needless to say, the government-aided private schools were blatant in practising untouchability in this matter.

In Muthusamypuram village (Tirunelveli), there is a government-aided Yadhavar Primary School. At its mid-day meal centre, in 2007, a woman named Arumugathai was appointed as a cook's assistant. She belonged to a Scheduled Caste. The district collector had made the appointment, but the secretary of the school refused to allow this worker to join. He said that he had not been consulted in the selection process. The woman registered a complaint with the collector, who sent a notice to the school management warning them that he would close the school if the woman was not allowed to join the mid-day meal centre.

The school secretary approached the High Court. After hearing the case, I decided that the secretary's action was wrong because it was caste-based. The problem was that if the collector's order was executed and the school was shut down, the future of hundreds of students would also be affected. Therefore, I dismissed the writ petition and ordered the secretary to allow the woman to join the centre without delay. In case he refused to obey, I directed the collector to take over the administration of the school. The following is the summary of my order:[5]

> The petitioner's high-handed behaviour in stopping a woman cook from a Dalit family from joining the noon-meal centre, for whatever reason, can never be condoned by this Court . . . This thoughtless action has put a question mark on the lunch of hundreds of children.
>
> The order of the District Collector stopping the Noon Meal Scheme has come to be challenged on grounds which are not legally sustainable. The fact that the views of the Management are taken into account for making the appointment does not mean that they have a veto power in the matter of selection of a candidate to the noon meal centre. The word 'consult' found in the G.O.Ms.No.294, Social Welfare & Nutritious Meal Programme (NMP.I) dated 21.10.1993, does not mean 'consent' from the School management . . . The grounds raised by the Management are ego-centric and arise out of social prejudice developed over the centuries which our Constitution is determined to eradicate.
>
> The Writ Petitioner, or Management, is directed to allow the Cook's Assistant, by name Mrs. Arumugathai, wife of the late Vellapandi of Muthusamypuram Village, residing

5 *The Secretary, Yadhavar Primary School, Muthusamiapuram, Ramasamyapuram-post vs District Collector, Tirunelveli District & Others*, W.P.(MD) No. 8462 of 2007 dated 12.10.2007. Judgment available on https://indiankanoon.org/doc/107585/ .

at Colony Street, Muthusamypuram, to join duty forthwith. The School Management are directed to allow the noon meal centre to be operational, more in the interest of the students than of the Management. The District Collector is also directed to ensure that the noon meal centre becomes operational, and he may direct the second respondent to visit the School and set right the problems created by the petitioner.

To return to the rule established in 1997, workers at the noon meal centres were selected from applicants living within a 1 km radius of the school. This was a denial of employment opportunity to Scheduled Caste women since the Dalit neighbourhoods are always located outside the villages. In 2007, Vasantha, an applicant to a job in a mid-day meal centre, found herself adversely affected by this rule and filed a petition pointing out the injustice. The criterion was effectively an assault on equal opportunity.

I heard this case and decided that the rule framed by the government violated the Constitution. In staff selection, only if two women obtained the same marks should the woman living closer to the centre be given preference. In my judgment, I said:[6]

If the contentions of the petitioners are to be accepted, then the preference should be given solely on the basis of residence, and that will be hit by Article 16(2) of the Constitution (against discrimination in employment on the basis of religion, race, caste, sex, descent, birthplace or place of residence]. However, considering the fact that the post requires constant attention towards the children and the availability of the person in a nearby area is preferable, the proximity of distance among the eligible candidates may be a constitutionally permissible factor. But the selection cannot be solely on the ground of residential preferences to the exclusion of other criteria (as] it will hit Article 16(2) of the Constitution. As rightly contended by the official respondents,

6 *P. Vasantha & Ors. vs District Collector, Dindigul District & Ors*, (2007) 6 MLJ 402. Judgment available on https://indiankanoon.org/doc/1056256/ .

the proximity of residence/locality is only a preference and not a qualification by itself. Once it is established that none of the selected candidates are otherwise disqualified, they cannot be edged out of consideration only on the ground that they were not residents of the locality.

> Further, preferring a candidate from a particular hamlet to the exclusion of candidates from other hamlets in the same Village Panchayat, or in respect of Panchayat Union Centres preferring the candidates from only one village to the exclusion of other villages living in the same panchayat union may also be arbitrary.

My judgment, in this case, was confirmed by a two-judge sitting in a writ appeal.[7] But the issue of reservation in employment for the mid-day meal centre remained unresolved. The government maintained that there could not be reservation for these posts. The state government made use of a central government circular issued in 2003 to justify the non-implementation of reservation. D. Pothumallee, a woman from Tiruvallur district, filed a petition against this. Between 2001 and 2009, she had applied six times for a job at the Anganwadi, only to be rejected each time. Her appeal was that in the appointment of staff in mid-day meals centres, reservation was not being followed, and the court should direct the government to follow reservation in staff selection.

As per the reservation policy, I observed that economic empowerment was not the only achievement in appointing a Dalit woman to a post, but a change in the social attitude towards Dalits would be brought about. Children eating the food cooked by a Dalit would enable the eradication of untouchability in the future. I ordered that the central government's circular in this matter need not be followed and that in Tamil Nadu, in all appointments to the

7 *S. Manjula vs The District Collector*, Sivangangai Dist., 2013(2) CWC 900.

noon-meal centres, a reservation roster must be implemented.

In this order, I quoted a US Supreme Court judgment that emphasized the necessity of bringing the socially marginalized black population into the mainstream. It observed:[8]

> We deal here with the right of all our children, whatever their race, to an equal start in life and to an equal opportunity to reach their full potential as citizens. Those children who have been denied that right in the past deserve better than to see fences thrown up to deny them that right in the future . . . [U] nless our children begin to learn together, there is little hope that our people will ever learn to live together.

I pointed out the necessity for reservation for Dalits and how it would bring about social change. I said:[9]

> It is needless to mention that such reservations will not only help economically empower the members of underprivileged sections of society, but will bring about the social integration of a civil society already fractured by communal and caste divisions. In the existing guidelines framed by the Government for filling up the post of workers under the Nutritious Meal scheme, as well as anganwadi workers, preference is given to residents of the village or to persons who are living within the same locality. In most cases, the schools or anganwadi centres are located in the hamlets dominated by upper castes. Applying preference as indicated in the guidelines will clearly edge out the members of Scheduled Castes from getting opportunities to work in such centres, since hardly any schools or anganwadi centres are situated in the dalit colonies. That was why the

8 *Milliken vs Bradley*, 418 U.S. 717, 783 (1974).

9 *Pothumallee D. vs District Collector, Collectorate, Tiruvarur District* (2010 (5) MLJ 46). Judgment available on https://www.legitquest.com/case/d-pothumallee-others-v-the-district-collector-thiruvarur-district-others/E0E5 .

Supreme Court also in the Right to Food case gave direction to the states to make efforts that all Scheduled Caste and Scheduled Tribe colonies in the country must have anganwadi centres. Such a direction may take years to achieve. Social integration can be achieved by providing reservation for the underprivileged sections of the society in such employment. That is why, by its interim orders in the Right to Food case, the Supreme Court had directed giving preference in employment of Dalits as cooks, helpers in such centres.

Feeding of children by members of the Scheduled Castes will go a long way in removing social disparities and practice of untouchability in different forms. The feeding of children belonging to different communities by a Dalit cook being resisted by the caste Hindus is another form of apartheid and it is not something new to this country. Even during the freedom struggle, controversies arose among the national leaders as noted above.

After bitter experiences, it was emphasized that by communal feasting and food being served to various groups by engaging cooks from underprivileged society will remove instantaneously some form of untouchability and 'will be a milestone in our march to an egalitarian society'

Chief Minister M. Karunanidhi, issued an order – G.O.Ms. No.142, Social Welfare Department, Govt. of Tamil Nadu, on 6 July 2010 – for the implementation of the rule of reservation for Dalits to positions in noon meal centres. By this order, nearly 25,000 Dalit women were given job opportunities in these centres.

8. THE SAD PLIGHT OF THE LIBRARY

Said a sheet of snow-white paper,
'Pure was I created, and pure will I remain forever.
I would rather be burnt and turn to white ashes than suffer darkness to touch me or
the unclean to come near me.'
The ink-bottle heard what the paper was saying, and
it laughed in its dark heart,
but it never dared to approach her.
And the multicoloured pencils heard her also,
and they too never came near her.
And the snow-white sheet of paper
did remain pure and chaste for ever
pure and chaste and empty.

– Kahlil Gibran

I felt compelled to quote this poem in a judgment, and the necessity arose in the following way. The Nallur panchayat of the Narikudi union in Virudhunagar district had decided to build a library under the Anna Marumalarchi (i.e., renaissance) scheme. K. Rajamani, a village resident who lived adjacent to the proposed site, appealed to the panchayat that the library should not be built there. The panchayat, where the majority belonged to the dominant caste of Thevars, backed out of its earlier decision. It passed a resolution on 2 January 2008 not to build the library within the village and sent it to the district collector for further action. Rajamani next approached the High Court, asking it to direct the collector to implement the panchayat resolution. He stated that if the library were built on the site, the passage to his house would be frequently obstructed. He also mentioned a drama hall near the chosen site where, on earlier occasions, clashes had occurred between the Adi Dravidars and other communities. On that basis, 'in the interests of the village people', he appealed to the court to order that the library be built elsewhere.

A lawyer named Jothi Basu brought the case before me in an innocuous-seeming manner. I told him that he had a duty not to appear in such matters with a name like his. He replied that he was only seeking formal relief for the resolution of the panchayat to be considered by the district collector. It seemed an innocent request, but I suspected a less innocent motive: that the majority Thevar community wanted to rescind the gram sabha's earlier decision on the location of the village library only because Dalits would frequent it to read books and newspapers. There was nothing innocent about the request, and it was plainly caste-biased. I told the lawyer that even if hundreds of people in Tamil Nadu were named after Jyoti Basu or any other leftist leader, I feared our situation would never change.

After hearing the case, I pointed out that Article 51-A of the Constitution has mandated certain fundamental duties for every citizen and that the petitioner's request went against this. I also observed that the panchayat resolution was motivated by the prejudice of the other communities in the village who did not want their area 'contaminated' and wished it to remain 'sacred'. I compared the mindset of the villagers to the white paper described in Kahlil Gibran's poem and quoted it in my judgment.

I also stated that the Collector would not be ordered to implement the panchayat resolution and dismissed the petition:[1]

> Further, in a writ petition filed under Article 226 of the Constitution of India, it is not in the realm of this Court to enforce every panchayat resolution even without looking

1 *K. Rajamani vs The District Collector, Virudhunagar Dist. & Ors*, W.P.(MD) No. 1034 of 2008 dt 4.8.2008.

into the substance of the resolution. In the present case, the undisguised motive of the petitioner and the 3rd respondent are that the Dalits (i.e. Adi Dravidars) will have free access to the street where a public library is to be situated and it will be an eyesore to the dominant community. Adding further fuel will be the fact they will actually read those books stacked in the library and may get more enlightened. No other logical or sensible reason to prevent the library's location can be gleaned from the affidavit. If the prayer of the petitioner is countenanced, that would run counter to Article 17 of the Constitution.[2]

2 Article 17 – Abolition of Untouchability: Untouchability is abolished and its practice in any form is forbidden. The enforcement of any disability arising out of Untouchability shall be an offence punishable in accordance with law.

9. THE PROBLEM WITH TOILETS

We are the children of the Indus Valley Civilisation. We can take pride in being the descendants of a people who constructed bathrooms and toilets 5000 years ago. None of us would have passed our history test without reading about Mohenjo-Daro and Harappa. Sixty-two kilometres away from Hyderabad in Pakistan, at a village called Lothal, excavations uncovered sewage channels made of baked mud. In the village of Harappa, they found bathrooms and toilets made of burnt clay. The excavations in Mohenjo-Daro revealed that there were attached toilets in the houses of the Dravidians of those times.

Oh, descendants of a glorious heritage! Tamil Nadu and the Tamil speaking people have fallen so low now! Why have you forgotten your history? Forty-two per cent of the people in the Asian–African countries have converted open spaces as toilets, and we bear the burden of infectious diseases and health hazards that result from that. A High Court asked such questions in a case. Now we will examine the case of the toilets.

There is a district munsif court in Ambattur. Two thousand members of the public visit this court every day, of whom two hundred are lawyers and twenty work in the court. Suddenly, one day in November 2006, the doors of the toilets in the court premises were locked. No one knew why. Renuka Devi, a woman lawyer who suffered this torture for a week, wrote a letter to the complaint box of a Tamil newspaper. I happened to read it and showed a translated version to Chief Justice A.P. Shah. We took it on file as a writ petition and summoned the commissioner of the Ambattur municipality. He appeared in court and offered his apology. His explanation was this. 'The municipality office had been shifted to a new building. The toilet was in the control of the old building. Since the person who had to maintain it had also been transferred, he locked the toilet and went away. This mistake was brought to my attention only after I received the notice from the High Court. Immediately I saw to it that the toilets were cleaned, the walls were white-washed, and the water tanks were filled with water and I have handed over the keys to the court.' In forty-eight hours, the High Court solved the problem by taking prompt action *suo motu*. And it was all because a woman lawyer expressed her anguish through a letter to the editor of a newspaper.

Mahatma Gandhi said that India lives in its villages. But even today, poor people living in thousands of villages have no proper toilet facilities. To set right this problem, schemes for building public toilets were framed in many villages with funds provided by the World Bank. Immediately, disputes arose regarding the location of the toilets since people vehemently objected that they should not be put up near their homes. The objections were taken up as writ petitions by the High Court. It is impossible to list all the cases. I will give you one sample.

Ayodhyapatinam is a village in the Salem district. The village panchayat resolved to build public toilets in the space available for use under the Anna Marumalarchi Scheme, and the panchayat entrusted the job to a contractor. A woman named Tamilarasi and two other villagers opposed it. The Court heard the case, dismissed it and confirmed the resolution of the Panchayat.[1] The court noted:

> . . . respondents have clearly demonstrated that there was necessity to build toilet as there were 50 Dalit families living in that area and further, the land in question was grama natham land. Sufficient safeguards have been taken to avoid any seepage and it is being constructed with modern ideas. (Para 25)... The petitioners' contention that the toilet was in the land owned by them is clearly found to be erroneous. . . The town

1 *R. Tamilarasi vs District Collector*, 2010 Writ L.R. 680 = 2010 (8) MLJ 662. Judgment available on https://indiankanoon.org/doc/452479/ .

panchayat is an elected body. Being conscious of the public need, especially of the Dalits, they have passed resolution unanimously to construct the toilets for needy people.

The court ordered that:

It is not for the petitioners to forestall such efforts made by respondent Panchayat. Since the construction is in advanced stage, the petitioners cannot challenge it on untenable grounds. The petitioners . . . came forward to challenge the action of the town panchayat taken pursuant to the resolution. The contentions raised by the petitioners cannot be accepted.

It is indeed amazing that persons living with attached bathrooms in their houses should oppose a scheme to construct public toilets. This is why this chapter commenced with the question of why a country that is a cradle of civilisation has fallen so low. The toilets had to be given police protection. In North Chennai, 225 toilets were constructed and maintained by the organization called Sulabh. However, the Chennai corporation cancelled the maintenance contract entered into with Sulabh. Immediately the members of the corporation who belonged to that area brought the toilets under their control and began to charge fees. The sanitary health workers opposed this and filed a case through their union. After hearing them, the Court ordered that the deputy commissioner of police take control of the 51 toilets taken over illegally by the councillors and ordered police protection to the toilets. A Tamil newspaper entertained itself by publishing a cartoon titled – 'the toilet guardians.'

There are no toilet facilities and no privacy in the women's sub-jail – these are small establishments at the sub-divisional level. A complaint was given in this regard to the Court. The Court took up the petition *suo motu* and appointed advocate Sudha Ramalingam as the advocate commissioner, directing her to visit the prisons of Tamil Nadu and file a report. Her report brought to light the darkness that prevailed in the jails of Tamil Nadu. On the basis of her report, the Court issued several directions to the government and prison authorities. One of them was for the immediate construction of toilets with water facility in all sub-jails and the construction of four-foot-high compound walls with doors to ensure privacy.[2] The government ordered the implementation of the Court's directions. There was a slight amelioration in the conditions of women prisoners.

An opinion poll conducted in the United States asked respondents to name the twentieth century's greatest invention. The answer was not nuclear power or television, or satellites. The unanimous vote was for the invention of the toilet. It is only because Chief Justice Gokhale (Madras High Court) understood the importance of toilets that a function was held in the court complex to inaugurate toilets on International Women's Day, 8 March 2010. A newspaper carried it, together with photographs. Even so, it is a matter of distress that there are not enough restrooms for the public who come in their thousands to the courts. In 2015, the state of Haryana took the unprecedented step of bringing an amendment to the Panchayati Raj Act, saying that only those who have toilets at home can contest in panchayat elections. The Supreme Court has also held that this amendment is valid.

2 Suo Motu Writ Petition No. 21243 of 2006 dt 18.3.2007 (DB).

10. INTER-CASTE MARRIAGE

Dr Ambedkar believed that inter-caste marriages would, to some extent, help weaken the caste system. At the same time, he knew that the inter-caste marriages and inter-caste feasts encouraged by committed reformists of Hinduism (including Gandhi) would not suffice to eradicate caste. He observed that the roots of the caste system were deeply embedded in the shastras, and unless belief in the shastras was destroyed, caste practices would not cease. The text of a speech he was prevented from giving in 1936, which he published the following year as *Annihilation of Caste*, expresses his thoughts on the subject:

> I am convinced that the real remedy is inter-marriage. Fusion of blood can alone create the feeling of being kith and kin, and unless this feeling of kinship, of being kindred, becomes paramount, the separatist feeling – the feeling of being aliens – created by caste will not vanish. Among the Hindus inter-marriage must necessarily be a factor of greater force in social life than it need be in the life of non-Hindus. Where society is already well knit by other ties, marriage is an ordinary incident of life. But where society is cut asunder, marriage as a binding force becomes a matter of urgent necessity. The real remedy for breaking caste is inter-marriage. Nothing else will serve as the solvent of the caste.[1]

It was necessary not just to break caste but pull it up by the root, as he added:

1 Ambedkar, B. R. 'The real key to destroying Caste is rejection of the Shastras' in *Annihilation of Caste: An Undelivered Speech*. https://ccnmtl.columbia.edu/projects/mmt/ambedkar/web/section_20.html .

> Criticizing and ridiculing people for not inter-dining or inter-marrying or occasionally holding inter-castes dinners and celebrating inter-caste marriages, is a futile method of achieving the desired end. The real remedy is to destroy the belief in the sanctity of the shastras.
>
> How do you expect to succeed, if you allow the shastras to continue to mould the beliefs and opinions of the people? Not to question the authority of the shastras– to permit the people to believe in their sanctity and their sanctions and to blame them and to criticize them for their acts as being irrational and inhuman – is an incongruous way of carrying on social reform. Reformers working for the removal of untouchability, including Mahatma Gandhi, do not seem to realize that the acts of the people are merely the results of their beliefs inculcated in their minds by the shastras and that people will not change their conduct until they cease to believe in the sanctity of the shastras on which their conduct is founded [. . .]
>
> To agitate for and to organize inter-caste dinners and inter-caste marriages is like forced feeding brought about by artificial means. Make every man and woman free from the thraldom of the shastras, cleanse their minds of the pernicious notions founded on the shastras, and he or she will inter-dine and inter-marry, without your telling him or her to do so.

It is a fact that when inter-caste marriages do take place, the newly married are hounded by their community. There are even 'honour killings'. In a matter like this, the case of *Lata Singh vs the State of UP and Anr.* (2006), the Supreme Court had expressed itself on the atrocities committed against couples in inter-caste marriages:

> There is no dispute that the petitioner is a major and was at all relevant times a major. Hence, she is free to marry anyone she likes or live with anyone she likes. There is no bar to an inter-

caste marriage under the Hindu Marriage Act or any other law. Hence, we cannot see what offence was committed by the petitioner, her husband, or her husband's relatives.

We are of the opinion that no offence was committed by any of the accused and the whole criminal case in question is an abuse of the process of the Court as well as of the administrative machinery at the instance of the petitioner's brothers who were only furious because the petitioner married outside her caste. We are distressed to note that instead of taking action against the petitioner's brothers for their unlawful and high-handed acts . . . the police has instead proceeded against the petitioner's husband and his relatives.

Since several such instances are coming to our knowledge of harassment, threats and violence against young men and women who marry outside their caste, we feel it necessary to make some general comments on the matter. The nation is passing through a crucial transitional period in our history, and this Court cannot remain silent in matters of great public concern, such as the present one.

The caste system is a curse on the nation and the sooner it is destroyed the better. In fact, it is dividing the nation at a time when we have to be united to face the challenges before the nation unitedly. Hence, inter-caste marriages are in fact in the national interest as they will result in destroying the caste system. However, disturbing news . . . from several parts of the country [reports] that young men and women who undergo inter-caste marriage, are threatened with violence, or violence is actually committed on them. In our opinion, such acts of violence or threats or harassment are wholly illegal and those who commit them must be severely punished. This is a free and democratic country, and once a person becomes a major he or she can marry whosoever he/she likes. If the parents of the boy or girl do not approve of such inter-caste or inter-religious marriage the maximum they can do is that they can

> cut off social relations with the son or the daughter, but they cannot [make] threats or commit or instigate acts of violence and cannot harass the person who undergoes such inter-caste or inter-religious marriage. We, therefore, direct that the administration/police authorities throughout the country will see to it that if any boy or girl who is a major undergoes inter-caste or inter-religious marriage with a woman or man who is a major, the couple are not harassed by anyone nor subjected to threats or acts of violence, and anyone who makes such threats or harasses or commits acts of violence, whether himself or at his instigation, is taken to task by instituting criminal proceedings by the police against such persons and further stern action is taken against such persons as provided by law. We sometimes hear of 'honour' killings of such persons who undergo inter-caste or inter-religious marriage of their own free will. There is nothing honourable in such killings, and in fact they are nothing but barbaric and shameful acts of murder committed by brutal, feudal-minded persons who deserve harsh punishment. Only in this way can we stamp out such acts of barbarism.[2]

Crimes against inter-caste marriage can generate ripples that travel far, claiming new victims. In 2013, such a case was before me. The previous year, a young man called Sivanesan, a diploma holder in mechanical engineering, had been denied appointment as a constable in the Tamil Nadu police department despite having cleared the written and physical tests and the medical examination. He was rejected because he had helped conduct an inter-caste marriage. Sivanesan's friend Sudhakar of Arani in Tiruvanamalai district and his classmate Arachelvi, who belonged to different communities, married in 2011. Both were adults and in love with each other. Theirs was not a case of dutiful sentiment such as

2 *Lata Singh vs State of UP and Anr.*, 2006 (5) SCC 475. Judgement available on https://indiankanoon.org/doc/1364215/ .

accompanies arranged marriages, but real love. Sivanesan was a witness at the registry of their marriage. Arachelvi's sister-in-law was a local sub-Inspector. With her help, a false case was registered against Sudhakar and Sivanesan – claiming that Arachelvi was a minor – and both men were sent to jail. Arachelvi produced documents proving that she was twenty-three years old at the time of her marriage. Sivanesan was released on bail. Later, Sudhakar submitted papers proving the legality of his marriage, and the FIR against him and Sivanesan was quashed. While the case was pending, Sivanesan was selected as a Grade II police constable. He was denied the job when a verification inquiry turned up his 'criminal background'. Sivanesan filed a writ petition which I heard. In my judgment, I quoted the Supreme Court judgment referred to above. I recorded that denying Sivanesan the police job was wrongful, and he must be given his appointment order.[3] The following is the order:

> In the present case, the Arni police, instead of helping the couples who got married, had not only filed a false case against the husband, but also against his friends who helped them to get married.
>
> In the light of the above background, the impugned order passed by the Superintendent of Police cannot be justified and hence it is set aside. The respondent is hereby directed to grant an appointment order to the petitioner within a period of three weeks from the date of receipt of copy of this order.

The Supreme Court has severely condemned the caste panchayats (in North India they are called khap panchayats) and severe action must be taken against them as per the Scheduled Caste and Scheduled Tribe (Prevention of Atrocities) Act. Here

3 *Sivanesan vs Superintendent of Police*, Tiruvannamalai Distt., (2013) 3 MLJ 142 (Mad) = 2013(1) CWC 845 = 2013(3) CTC 226 = 2013(2) LLN 434 (Mad). Judgment available on https://indiankanoon.org/doc/3008563/ .

is an extract from a judgment delivered in 2011, in the case of *Arumugam Servai vs the State of Tamil Nadu*:

> We have in recent years heard of 'khap panchyats' (known as katta panchayats in Tamil Nadu) which often decree or encourage honour killings or other atrocities in an institutionalized way on boys and girls of different castes and religion who wish to get married, or have been married; or interfere with the personal lives of people. We are of the opinion that this is wholly illegal and has to be ruthlessly stamped out. As already stated in Lata Singh's case, there is nothing honourable in honour killing or other atrocities and, in fact, it is nothing but barbaric and shameful murder. Other atrocities in respect of personal lives of people committed by brutal, feudal minded persons deserve harsh punishment. Only in this way can we stamp out such acts of barbarism and feudal mentality. Moreover, these acts take the law into their own hands, and amount to kangaroo courts, which are wholly illegal.[4]

I was happy that I was able to help one man who had helped his friend to have an inter-caste marriage.

4 *Arumugam Servai vs State of Tamil Nadu*, 2011(6) SCC 405. Judgment available on https://indiankanoon.org/doc/1337458/ .

11. POTHUMBU GIRLS

When the first prime minister of India, Pandit Jawaharlal Nehru, was asked which of his government's achievements he considered the foremost, he replied that it was women's education. He was one of the national leaders who believed that India would progress only if women were educated. We now see many women in educational institutions, and, in fact, the women perform much better than men.

Given these facts, it shocked everyone when, in 2011, the villagers of Pothumbu near Madurai, Tamil Nadu, said that they would not send their girl children to school anymore. The reason was even more shocking. It was because of the bestial conduct of the headmaster of the Podumbu Government High School. Over his three years at the school, he had sexually abused more than a hundred girls in his care. When the little girls began to share their horror stories with their parents, the entire village shuddered. They staged a protest. Brinda Karat, the President of All-India Democratic Women's Association (AIDWA), conducted a direct inquiry and found that the complaints were genuine.

Ponnuthai, the district secretary of AIDWA in the Madurai Rural District, and the parents of the affected students lodged a complaint at the police station, but to no effect. A relative of the headmaster was a teacher at the same school. Other relatives were teachers in nearby schools. They threatened the complainants and verbally abused the affected students. Later, a fact-finding committee headed by U. Nirmala Rani, a Madurai-based advocate, went to the village. Some of the students had completed their school education by then. Some had even got married. And some were afraid that if they gave evidence, they might face problems. The fact-finding committee tried its best and conducted an inquiry among the students, parents, and teachers. This committee's report first brought to light the full extent of the horrors committed by the headmaster. It listed the sexual harassment and violence inflicted by him. He would ask sick students to come to his room and, telling them he would pray for their recovery, he would touch their breasts as if marking them with the sign of the cross. He would call students in private and hug them. Under the excuse of looking for something, he would insert his hand under their clothes. He also forced some of the children to hold his penis. He would ask the younger girls to sit on his lap and do unspeakable things to them. He got students to sweep the floor and took pictures of them bent over. It is sickening to list these horrible acts.

Veerasamy, the father of one of the affected girls, filed a case with the Madurai bench of Madras High Court. He requested that a special investigating team be constituted to investigate this history of sexual abuse and award compensation to his daughter. AIDWA impleaded itself in this petition. As a first step, the court directed the involvement of the Child Welfare Committee under the Protection of Child Rights Act and directed this committee to file a report. The Child Welfare Committee's report corroborated the charges filed by the Fact-Finding Committee headed by U. Nirmala Rani. The High Court was not happy when it examined the records submitted by the police department in respect of the inquiry conducted by them.

It ordered the Madurai district police superintendent to appear in person. Accordingly, Mr Asra Garg, the superintendent of police, appeared in court. In the meantime, the education department temporarily suspended the headmaster. The police arrested him. Since nobody opposed the grant of bail strongly, he was let out. A relative and a friend who had assisted him were transferred to far-off schools.

The High Court found that a number of the abused children belonged to the SC community. It ordered that the matter be registered under the SC & ST (Prevention of Atrocities) Act, 1989.

Further, a woman officer of the rank of assistant superintendent should be appointed, that the government appoint a woman special public prosecutor, and an inquiry be conducted under the direct supervision of the district police superintendent. The court stated:

> In this case, admittedly, [a] number of school children [who] belonged to SC community were sexually exploited by the headmaster of the school. Admittedly, the complaints of the children and their parents, if proved, would attract Section 3(1)(xi) and (xii) of the SC and ST (Prevention of Atrocities) Act, 1989. Therefore, in such circumstances, the investigation can be done by an officer not below the rank of Deputy Superintendent of Police . . . In this case, it should be done by a woman police officer who is not below the rank of the Deputy Superintendent of Police.

The High Court ordered that protection be given to the affected girls and care taken that they should not feel threatened when their statements were recorded. The court directed that the girls be given counselling and whether they were SC or non-SC, the district collector should offer them a compensation of Rs 1,20,000 each, without waiting for the end of the trial. As soon as the case is registered, the special court should take into account the nature of the case and conclude it expeditiously. The recording of evidence with the girls must be done with sensitivity, and the accused teachers must be transferred to far-off schools and on no account should they return to the Podumbu school.

The court recorded the widespread child sexual abuse and that steps should be taken to remove it. It also stated that:

> [T]he District Collector, Madurai is hereby directed to identify the number of girls from out of the three reports, . . . finding team report headed by Ms U. Nirmala Rani, report by the Child Welfare Committee, and statements given by the children and

their parents to the then Investigating Officer and prepare the initially report of those names. (Para 17.3)

The inquiry continued even after the judgment; the twenty-four students who complained were given Rs 28,80,000 as compensation in the first stage. Yet, many students feared the stigma if they were identified and did not come forward to make a complaint. The court ordered:

> There may be other children who have not come forward to make a complaint. In such a case, if any complaint is made directly to the District Collector, even those complaints can be entertained by him to award compensation after finding the veracity of the complaints and if there is any prima facie case, not only should the District Collector grant compensation, but also refer those complaints for further investigation by the Investigating Officer.

The High Court directed that if students came forward to complain even at a later date, they should be given compensation after verification. The government paid a total of Rs 66 lakhs as compensation. Since the judgement, the Podumbu Government High School has returned to normalcy. The girls now go there to study. Nehru's dream must come true.[1]

1 *M.Veerasamy vs State of Tamil Nadu*, 2012(3) CTC 641. Judgment available on https://indiankanoon.org/doc/169773352/ .

12. RIGHT TO FOOD HABIT

Food habits are the choice of an individual. To convert one's choice into a religious diktat against others is unacceptable, for it only leads to division among human beings. It was common for brahmins in Vedic times to consume meat, and even today, some brahmin sects in north India eat mutton and fish. It is pointless to cover up this fact and attempt to turn the entire society towards vegetarianism. The World Vegetarian Congress, founded in 1908, sought VIP converts to vegetarianism to speak at its gatherings and propagate the message that vegetarianism is the right way of life. Doing this alienated many who did not share these values, especially as the tactic smacked of elitism, of browbeating others into submission. It may be recalled here that the Madras Animals and Birds Sacrifices Act had been in the law books since 1950. The cultural anthropologist Anthony Good notes the unresolved tension at the heart of this law: it was framed and enacted within months of India's new Constitution but could not be implemented.[1] Drafted in accordance with elite opinion and priorities, the new law enjoyed little support on the ground. In 1969, it was renamed the Tamil Nadu Animals and Birds Sacrifices Prevention Act, but its existence remained purely formal. When the state government under J. Jayalalithaa suddenly decided to enforce this law in 2003, and it met with furious opposition. The government was compelled not only to withdraw the enforcement but repeal the Act altogether. This was because public opinion in Tamil Nadu viewed the government's actions as favouring upper-caste groups

1 Good A., 'Animal Sacrifice and the Law in Tamil Nadu, South India.' Paper presented at 5e Congrès Asie et Pacifique, Paris, September 2015. https://www.sps.ed.ac.uk/sites/default/files/assets/pdf/Sacrifice_and_the_law_in_Tamil_Nadu.pdf .

and an agenda of Hindutva against the traditions of rural and subordinate-caste communities.

In his book, *The Untouchables: Who Were They and Why They Became Untouchables* (1948), Ambedkar had written:

> The Census returns show that the meat of the dead cow forms the chief item of food consumed by communities which are generally classified as Untouchable communities. No Hindu community, however low, will touch cow's flesh. On the other hand, there is no community which is really an Untouchable community which has not something to do with the dead cow. Some eat her flesh, some remove the skin, some manufacture articles out of her skin and bones.
>
> From the survey of the Census Commissioner, it is well established that Untouchables eat beef. The question however is: Has beef-eating any relation to the origin of Untouchability? Or is it merely an incident in the economic life of the Untouchables? Can we say that the Broken Men came to be treated as Untouchables because they ate beef? There need be no hesitation in returning an affirmative answer to this question. No other answer is consistent with facts as we know them.
>
> In the first place, we have the fact that the Untouchables or the main communities which compose them eat the dead cow and those who eat the dead cow are tainted with Untouchability and no others. The co-relating between Untouchability and the use of the dead cow is so great and so close that the thesis that it is the root of Untouchability seems to be incontrovertible. In the second place if there is anything that separates the Untouchables from the Hindus, it is beef-eating. Even a superficial view of the food taboos of the Hindus will show that there are two taboos regarding food which serve as dividing lines. There is one taboo against meat-

> eating. It divides Hindus into vegetarians and flesh-eaters. There is another taboo which is against beef-eating. It divides Hindus into those who eat cow's flesh and those who do not. From the point of view of Untouchability the first dividing line is of no importance. But the second is. For it completely marks off the Touchables from the Untouchables. The Touchables whether they are vegetarians or flesh-eaters are united in their objection to eat cow's flesh. As against them stand the Untouchables who eat cow's flesh without compunction and as a matter of course and habit.[2]

Ambedkar concludes that the 'Broken Men were exposed to scorn and contempt on the ground that they were Buddhists and the main cause of their Untouchability was beef-eating.'

From 1993 onwards, the Gujarat state government and the Ahmedabad Municipal Corporation had intermittently ordered butcher shops in the state to close for periods ranging from eight to eighteen days, the period of Paryushan, of fasting by the Jains. The butchers went to court opposing this. In 2008, a two-judge bench of Justices H.K. Sema and M. Katju at the Supreme Court dismissed their case. It held that the motive of the corporation's order was to avoid hurting the sentiments of a minority community and a temporary closure order was not wrong. The judgment added that the ban was imposed for a limited period, and the government cannot otherwise dictate to people what their food habits should be throughout the year, these being a matter of individual freedom. People used to buying meat from butcher shops within the corporation limits could not be expected to go to distant places to buy it. Here is an extract from the judgment:

> We have to take a practical review of the matter. Most people

2 *The Essential Writings of B.R. Ambedkar*, edited by Valerian Rodrigues, Oxford University Press, 2002, pp. 403-405.

do not have the money to purchase meat from other cities or other states and bring it to Ahmedabad. Almost all meat-eaters get their meat from the local butcher shop in the city, usually from a shop which is close to their residence. Hence, closure of the slaughterhouse, in substance, means compelling the non-vegetarians to become vegetarians for 9 days.[3]

In Tamil Nadu, a few families of the Arunthathiyar community used to put up beef shops at the weekly market at Kavundapadi near Erode. They had been doing so for over forty years when, in 2012, the panchayat president ordered the closure of their shops. Opposing this, the convener of the Joint Committee for Eradication of Castes tried to organize a protest demonstration. The deputy superintendent of police stopped the demonstration. The case registered by those opposing his action came to me for hearing. In my judgment, I referred to the fight against Hindu religious rituals and the forcing of food habits on people. I said in my order:

> It has to be seen whether the stand taken by the respondents [the DSP, panchayat, and administration] is justified. No doubt, the persons who were running beef stalls belonged to the arunthathiyar community. Traditionally they were doing such business, as claimed by the petitioner, for over four decades. Merely because they happen to be arunthathiyars and wanted to conduct a protest demonstration against the decision of the panchayat [led the DSP to assume that it would] automatically lead to a communal fight. This is only a futile imagining of the first respondent. In fact, Dr Ambedkar, who was a champion of the rights of the downtrodden had occasion to consider protests by Scheduled Caste people against members of the

3 *Hinsa Virodhak Sangh vs Mirzapur Moti Kuresh Jamat* reported in 2008 (5) SCC 33.

Hindu religion who followed chathurvarna (the four-caste system) and who treated the Scheduled Castes as avarna (no caste). It was stated that mere peaceful protest is not [a threat] and it is fair to participate in such event.[4]

My judgment quoted from Dr Ambedkar's distinction of the interests of Dalits from the savarnas:

> Now the Oppressed Classes must not spend money and manpower fruitlessly and must stop the fight on Satyagraha front. They must now consider their society separate from the Hindu society and organize the former to obtain for it an independent and respectable place in the country. Henceforth, all Depressed Classes must not take part in any Hindu religious festivals, Ratha, worships and other similar occasions.[5]

Addressing a gathering in Bombay in May 1936, Ambedkar spoke in Marathi, clarifying an intention he had declared the previous year – of converting to another religion. He referred to the enduring struggle between the Hindus and the Untouchables as a permanent phenomenon, lines that I went on to quote in my judgment, employing Vasant Moon's translation:

> To put it straight, it can be said that the struggle between Hindus and the Untouchables is a permanent phenomenon. It is eternal, because the religion which has placed you at the lowest level of the society is itself eternal, according the belief of the caste-Hindu people. No change according to times and

4 *S. Veerakumar vs The Deputy Superintendent of Police*, Gobi Sub Division, Gobichettipalayam, Erode District., (2012) 5 MLJ 1039). Judgment available on https://indiankanoon.org/doc/109349370/ .

5 Rev Dr K. David Pandyan, *Dr B.R. Ambedkar and the Dynamics of Neo-Buddhism*, New Delhi, 1996, p. 80. See also Ambedkar's statement of 14 February 1933 on the Temple Entry Bill proposed by Ranga Iyer, in *Dr Babasaheb Ambedkar: Writings and Speeches*, Vol. 17, Part 1, pp. 195–200.

> circumstances is possible. You are at the lowest rung of the ladder today. You shall remain lowest forever. This means the struggle between Hindus and Untouchables shall continue forever.[6]

As to the nature of the fight by the Scheduled Caste people against religious fanatics in the Hindu religion, he had described the fight as one for changing the mind of the Hindus. Further, he had stated that it is not a mere question of temple entry, but a struggle to change the Hindu mindset and had added:

> Your problems will not be solved by temple entry. Politics, economics, education, religion all are part of the problem. Today's satyagraha is a challenge to the Hindu mind. Are the Hindus ready to consider us men or not; we will discover this today . . . We know that the god in the temple is of stone. Darsan and puja will not solve our problems. But we will start out, and try to make a change in the minds of the Hindus.[7]

These lines are taken from his address to a gathering at Nashik on 2 March 1930 at the launch of the Kala Ram temple-entry movement, undertaken by B.K. Gaikwad (1902–71). Quoting the passages above, I gave permission for the Committee's protest demonstration and overruled the administration's excuse for its ban on the protest, that it would endanger communal peace. I said in my order:

> [T]he reasons set out by the first respondent cannot be accepted as valid. This court does not think that there will be any communal [or] religious division between Dalits and

6 'Dr B.R. Ambedkar: Why Conversion?' in *B.R. Ambedkar: Political Thinkers of Modern India*, edited by Verinder Grover, New Delhi: 1993, p. 4.

7 E. Zelliot, *Ambedkar's World: The Making of Babasaheb and the Dalit Movement*, New Delhi: Navayana, 2004, p. 88.

rest of Hindu followers in the said village. On the other hand, the need of agitation is only against the ban by the panchayat on running the beef stall, thereby jeopardizing the interest of persons who are traditionally carrying on the said trade.

13. COMPENSATION FOR ATROCITIES BY THE POLICE

Dismissing an appeal filed by one Arumugam Servai in 2011, the Supreme Court passed an order directing the government and the police department to take severe action against atrocities perpetrated on the Scheduled Castes and Scheduled Tribes. Copies of the order were sent to the High Courts and all the government officials concerned for further action. Here is an extract:

> [W]e direct the administrative and police officials to take strong measures to prevent such atrocious acts. If any such incidents happen, apart from instituting criminal proceedings against those responsible for such atrocities, the State Government is directed to immediately suspend the District Magistrate/ Collector and SSP/SPs of the district as well as other officials concerned and charge-sheet them and proceed against them departmentally if they do not (1) prevent the incident if it has not already occurred but they have knowledge of it in advance, or (2) if it has occurred, they do not promptly apprehend the culprits and others involved and institute criminal proceedings against them, as in our opinion they will be deemed to be directly or indirectly accountable in this connection.
>
> The appellants in the present case have behaved like uncivilized savages, and hence deserve no mercy. With these observations the appeals are dismissed.
>
> Copy of this judgment shall be sent to all Chief Secretaries, Home Secretaries and Directors General of Police in all States and Union Territories of India with the direction that it should be circulated to all officers up to the level of District

> Magistrates and S.S.P./S.P. for strict compliance. Copy will also be sent to the Registrars General/Registrars of all High Courts who will circulate it to all Hon'ble Judges of the Court.[1]

The reason parliament enacted the Scheduled Castes and Scheduled Tribes (Prevention of Atrocities) Act, 1989, can be seen from the 'Objects and Reasons' that were stated with the act:

> Because of the awareness created amongst the Scheduled Castes and the Scheduled Tribes through spread of education, etc., they are trying to assert their rights and this is not being taken very kindly by the others. When they assert their rights and resist practices of untouchability against them or demand statutory minimum wages or refuse to do any bonded and forced labour, the vested interests try to cow them down and terrorize them. When the Scheduled Castes and the Scheduled Tribes try to preserve their self-respect or honour of their women, they become irritants for the dominant and the mighty. Occupation and cultivation of even the Government allotted lands by the Scheduled Castes and the Scheduled Tribes is resented and more often these people become victims of attacks by the vested interests.[2]

P. Kalimuthu, former director-general of police of Tamil Nadu, exposed the pathetic way in which the Prevention of Atrocities Act is being implemented. In his Foreword to a book in Tamil by A. Jaison, Kalimuthu says:

> Cases are not registered on time after atrocities against the Scheduled Castes – who also hesitate to register police

1 *Arumugam Servai vs State of Tamil Nadu*, 2011 (6) SCC 405. Judgement available at: https://indiankanoon.org/doc/1337458/ .

2 *Objects and Reasons: SC and ST (Prevention of Atrocities) Act, 1989*, Professional Book Publishers, 2003, p. 1.

complaints for fear of social isolation and revenge. Even when cases are registered, the attitude of the police is indifference. Political interference and money power also prevent the police from acting honestly and independently. With the few registered complaints, there is hardly any honest investigation. The cases never reach the court within a reasonable time schedule . . .

Also, the delays in the judicial procedures have weakened the Scheduled Caste and Scheduled Tribe (Prevention of Atrocities) Act. In the time lag between the registry of the case and the hearing there is a risk of witnesses turning hostile; and fear among petitioners threatened by the upper castes further weakens their case. The affected people, who have to wait very long for justice, eventually lose interest in the case. In cases registered under Scheduled Caste and Scheduled Tribe (Prevention of Atrocities) Act, 1989, less than 3 per cent ended in conviction. Such statistics encourage casteists and the incidence of atrocities against Scheduled Castes and Scheduled Tribes increases every year . . .

The action taken by the Government to prevent atrocities against the Scheduled Castes and Scheduled Tribes thus ends in failure. Although the protective laws, compensation, and development programmes provisioned by the Constitution have helped to some extent, they have not had the desired results. The indifference of the politicians, the partiality practised by officials and the hostility of society are factors that prevent the law from achieving its intended objective.[3]

From time to time, some members of the dominant castes have demanded the repeal of the Atrocities Act. In the Rajasthan

3 P. Kalimuthu I.P.S. (Retd. DGP), Foreword to *Vankodumai Thaduppu Sattathai Theeviramaga Amalpaduthuveer* (Tamil), A. Jaison, Annai Ramabhai Publications, 2012. My translation.

High Court and a few other high courts, cases were filed that the law be declared unconstitutional, cases that were transferred to the Supreme Court where they were all dismissed. Subsequently, the ambit of the Act was enlarged by parliament, only to be weakened again in 2018 by the Supreme Court's judgment in the Subhash Kashinath Mahajan case (referred to earlier; see Preface). Fortunately, Parliament amended the Act yet again, and the Supreme Court nullified its 2018 decision. However, the Atrocities Act faces continual attrition from a police force reluctant to register offences, shoddy investigation, and also judicial apathy. The abuse of Dalits and Adivasis is based on a presumed caste superiority and a desire to humiliate them, yet the Supreme Court ruled in November 2020 that abusive terms that do not explicitly involve caste slurs are not offences covered by the Act. In May the same year, the Punjab and Haryana High Court ruled that abuse delivered on the phone, even caste slurs, are not in public view and hence fall outside the provisions of the Act.[4] The National Crime Records Bureau reveals that crimes against Dalits and Adivasis have been increasing steeply – by 9.4 and 9.3 per cent, respectively, between 2019 and 2020.[5] Further, a 2019 study found that one in three prisoners in India is either a Dalit or an Adivasi, the majority of them unconvicted.[6]

On 19 September 1999, at Vayalapadi village of Kunnam

4 Sharma. S. (2020) Home Case Briefs P&H Hc | 'No Offence Constituted Under Sc/St Act Where Abusive Language In The Name Of Caste Used Over Phone Call: Criminal Proceedings Against Accused.' June 1, 2020. https://www.scconline.com/blog/post/2020/06/01/ph-hc-no-offence-constituted-under-sc-st-act-where-abusive-language-in-the-name-of-caste-used-over-phone-call-criminal-proceedings-against-accused-quashed/ .

5 PTI (2021) 'Crimes against SCs, STs went up in 2020; UP, MP top charts: NCRB data.' *Business Standard*. https://www.business-standard.com/article/current-affairs/crimes-against-scs-sts-went-up-in-2020-up-mp-top-charts-ncrb-data-121091601048_1.html .

6 The Wire Staff (2019) 'One in Every Three Under-Trial Prisoners in India Is Either SC or ST: Study', *The Wire*. https://thewire.in/rights/one-in-every-three-under-trial-prisoners-in-india-is-either-sc-or-st-study .

taluka in Perambalur district, the police attacked the people of the Dalit colony without warning. Lands had been acquired for the use of the Dalits under the T. N. Acquisition of Land for Harijans Welfare Schemes Act, 1978. When the previous owners of these lands attempted to plant saplings there, the Dalits opposed them. Taking the side of the previous landowners, the police forcibly entered the colony and attacked – even the old, women, and children weren't spared. Following an inquiry by the tahsildar, four police personnel were suspended, but no criminal case was registered against them. The four policemen approached the court to get the suspension orders against them revoked. One of these cases came to the Madurai Bench in 2006, and the other three went to the Principal Bench of Chennai. I heard the case in Madurai and asked why the government had not registered cases against the four policemen under the Prevention of Atrocities Act. Before dismissing the case, I gave the following direction:

> The Government accepted the report of the inquiry conducted under PSO 151 and also the recommendations of the district collector to initiate departmental action against the police personnel who were responsible for the forcible entry into village colony and attacking the women and children on 19.9.1999. It was also stated that disciplinary proceedings against those persons should be completed within a time limit prescribed. It is not clear as to why the Government did not initiate action in terms of the Scheduled Castes and the Scheduled Tribes (Prevention of Atrocities) Act, 1989 by launching criminal prosecution under Section 3 of the Act . . .
>
> The report under PSO 151 cannot be lightly brushed aside. In the present context as many as 86 witnesses were examined including the women and children of the adi-dravidar colony. A perusal of the evidence adduced by them makes for sad reading . . .

> In order to protect identify of the witnesses, their names are not mentioned here. But, one woman whose evidence is given at page 10 of the report stated that her son, who was 21 years old and paralytic could not walk since 4 ½ years [of age], was attacked by the raiding party. When she attempted to prevent the police from attacking her son, she was also beaten. Another woman from the Dalit colony, whose evidence is found in page 145, stated that her own children were beaten up by the police. A boy who was a student of X- Standard was brutally attacked and kept in a Sub-jail for 46 days even though he was a juvenile. Another witness at page 175 said she was a pregnant woman, and she was kicked by the booted legs of the police . . .
>
> Even the concerned tahsildar, deputy tahsildar and VAO have deposed about the police brutality in the colony. It is not as if the women and children were part of any rioting mob. But the police went in a group into the Dalit colony at about 7.00 p.m. and attacked the unarmed women, children and infirm. When such brutalities take place, the State cannot be mute spectator to the said issue and should take necessary curative action.[7]

In June 1992, over 260 police and forest department personnel, along with six revenue officials, forcibly entered the tribal village of Vachathi in Dharmapuri district and brutally attacked the people. It was purportedly an action against sandalwood smuggling and to seek leads on the whereabouts of the outlaw Veerappan. However, the raiding party ransacked the settlement of the forest dwellers, killed their cattle, destroyed houses and assaulted a hundred people. Eighteen women were raped. It took more than a fortnight

7 *J. Thangappan vs Superintendent of Police, Thanjavur*. W.P.(MD)No. 3614 of 2006 dated 5.10.2007, *R. Subramanian & Ors. vs Superintendent of Police*, W.P.16959 of 2007 and batch cases dated 24.10.2007.

for the news to reach the public. Initially, the government of the day, headed by J. Jayalalithaa, denied that such a raid had taken place. When that was disproved, the forest minister claimed the village was a den of sandalwood smugglers. As late as August 1992, the police refused to register a case filed by the 18 rape survivors who, after being repeatedly raped, were photographed before piles of sandalwood, following which the photographs were shown to a district magistrate who remanded the women to police custody.

The Madras High Court ordered an inquiry by, B. Bhamathi, the director of the state SC/ST commission. Upon being informed in 1993 that there was evidence for the accusations against the officials, the court ordered that a departmental inquiry be conducted and criminal cases registered against them. The case was transferred to the CBI investigation in 1995. Twelve of the accused policemen approached the High Court with the plea that the departmental inquiry should not be conducted before the criminal cases against them were heard. I heard this case in 2009 and issued the following order:

> Considering that the petitioners were charged for grave offences such as raping tribal women, the question of stalling the departmental action cannot indefinitely be postponed. In the light of the above factual matrix and the legal precedents cited above, this writ petition stands dismissed.[8]

In 2012 – twenty years after the atrocity – sentencing took place in the Vachathi case, with 269 officials being convicted, 17 of them for rape. By this time, 54 of the convicted officials were dead.

Another case of this nature came to me in 2013. It concerned policemen praying that their suspension – on the accusation

8 *V. Jagannathan & Ors. vs DIG of Police, Vellore Range Vellore*, W. P. 34670 of 2006 dated 30.09.2009. Judgement available on https://www.casemine.com/judgement/in/56090437e4b014971115d8aa .

that they had raped Dalit women – be revoked. On the night of 22 November 2011, at the Manampoondi outer ring road in Thirukoilur taluk, four Dalit women were returning home from work. A police inspector, a sub-inspector, a head constable, and two constables on this beat raped these women. The women registered a police complaint, and the DIG of the Villupuram Division suspended the five personnel. In addition, cases were registered against them under the Indian Penal Code, and the Scheduled Caste and Scheduled Tribe (Prevention of Atrocities) Act at the Thirukoilur Police Station. While the case was pending, the policemen filed writ petitions praying that their suspension be revoked.

I heard the case and passed the following judgment:

> [U]nless the police files a final report before the trial court and the trial court proceeds to conduct the trial in terms of the final report, at the maximum, the petitioners can make use of the said report as defence. It is not clear, even whether the said defences are open to them, in the light of the provisions of the SC & ST (Prevention of Atrocities) Act, 1989 and in the light of Section 114-A of the Indian Evidence Act and that question has to be decided by the trial court . . .
>
> The orders of suspension have been passed by the highest authority, namely Inspector General of Police (North Zone), in charge of Deputy Inspector General of Police, Villupuram Range. If the petitioners had contended that he was in excess of his jurisdiction, this Court does not think that such a stand is commensurate with the Tamil Nadu Police Subordinate Service (Discipline and Appeal) Rules. It suffices that the highest authority is entitled to suspend a person, who was working as a Subordinate Police Officer. The fact that no charge memo is issued, cannot improve the case of the petitioners, as the suspension has been made since the criminal case has

been launched against them. Since the petitioners are accused of serious offences against the women and the women belong to SC & ST and the Police are investigating the case, this Court is not inclined to interfere with the orders of suspension.[9]

9 *R. Srinivasan & Ors vs Superintendent of Police, Villupuram Dist., Villupuram & Ors*, 2013 (1) MLJ (Crl) 286. Judgement available on https://www.legitquest.com/case/r-srinivasan-others-v-the-superintendent-of-police-villupuram-district-others/78691 .

14. BREAKING THE WALL OF UNTOUCHABILITY

In the United States, several human rights movements have fought the racism against African Americans. Although the Constitution had proclaimed that all men are equal, for more than two centuries, a form of apartheid continued in practice. Even after the abolition of slavery in 1865, two Americas remained visible on the ground, where Black people did not secure franchise till the Voting Rights Act of 1965. During the hundred years between these two landmark events, the doctrine of 'separate but equal' preserved racial inequality in a constitutional guise. Segregated public facilities were the norm; they included separate schools for white and Black children. To put an end to this practice – which started at the elementary school level – a class action lawsuit was eventually filed in the U.S. Supreme Court. The court's 1954 judgment in *Brown vs the Board of Education of Topeka* was historic and has come to be known worldwide. With a unanimous 9–0 decision, the court declared that all schools in America must admit children without discrimination based on colour. The court reinforced desegregation in subsequent rulings – *Green vs County School Board* (1968) and *Swann vs Charlotte-Mecklenburg Board of Education* (1971) – which mandated programmes to bus black children to predominantly white schools in order to achieve racial integration.[1]

The implementation of the court's order was delayed by appeals and by a tacit ground-level resistance that continued

1 Law Library - American Law and Legal Information 'School Desegregation: The Busing Debate'. https://law.jrank.org/pages/10024/School-Desegregation-BUSING-DEBATE.html .

for years. However, a blow for equality had been struck in 1954, and in its aftermath, the anti-racist movement continued to gain ground. Thurgood Marshall (1908–1993), a Black lawyer who had represented the human rights activists in the Brown case, later became the first African American judge of the Supreme Court, but social progress did not run smooth. In 1978 he found himself isolated on the bench in yet another case concerning racism against black people. The case, *Regents of the University of California vs Bakke* – known today as the Bakke decision – saw the U.S. Supreme Court uphold affirmative action but invalidate the use of racial quotas. In a dissenting opinion, Marshall wrote:

> It is unnecessary in 20th century America to have individual Negroes demonstrate that they have been victims of racial discrimination; the racism of our society has been so pervasive that none, regardless of wealth or position, has managed to escape its impact. The experience of Negroes in America has been different in kind, nor just in degree, from that of other ethnic groups. It is not merely the history of slavery alone but also that a whole people were marked as inferior by the law. And that mark has endured. The dream of America as the great melting pot has not been realized for the Negro; because of his skin colour he never even made it into the pot.[2]

We have already seen Rosa Parks' famous Montgomery protest against segregation and racial entitlement in public transport. Martin Luther King Jr, had addressed a gathering of nearly 5,000 people at the Holt Street Baptist Church in Montgomery on 5 December 1955, four days after Rosa Parks' arrest, where he praised 'the boundless outreach of her integrity', adding:

2 The Bakke, 438 U.S. at 400 (Marshall, J.,) quoted in *All Deliberate Speed* by Charles J. Ogletree, Jr., W. W. Norton & Company, New York & London (2004), p. 326.

> You know, my friends, there comes a time when people get tired of being trampled over by the iron feet of oppression. There comes a time, my friends, when people get tired of being plunged across the abyss of humiliation, where they experience the bleakness of nagging despair. There comes a time when people get tired of being pushed out of the glittering sunlight of life's July, and left standing amid the piercing chill of an alpine November . . .
>
> And we are not wrong. We are not wrong in what we are doing. If we are wrong, the Supreme Court of this nation is wrong. If we are wrong, the Constitution of the United States is wrong. If we are wrong God Almighty is wrong. If we are wrong, Jesus of Nazareth was merely a utopian dreamer that never came down to earth. And we are determined here in Montgomery to work and fight until justice runs down like water and righteousness like a mighty stream.[3]

Eight years later, King was held in the city jail of Birmingham, Alabama, after taking part in protests and sit-ins against racial segregation. From his cell, he wrote a long 'open letter' – scribbled on pieces of toilet paper and in the margins of newspapers which had to be smuggled out piecemeal – to address a group of white clergymen who had criticized him for 'unwise and untimely demonstrations':

> Perhaps it is easy for those who have never felt the stinging darts of segregation to say, 'Wait.' But when you have seen vicious mobs lynch your mothers and fathers at will and drown your sisters and brothers at whim; when you have seen hate-filled policemen curse, kick, and even kill your black brothers and sisters; when you see the vast majority of your

3 Meltzer, Milton. *There Comes a Time: The Struggle for Civil Rights* (2000), Random House, New York; pp. 77, 93, and 94.

> twenty million Negro brothers smothering in an airtight cage of poverty in the midst of an affluent society . . .
>
> When you are forever fighting a degenerating sense of 'nobodiness'– then you will understand why we find it difficult to wait. There comes a time when the cup of endurance runs over, and men are no longer willing to be plunged into the abyss of despair. I hope, sirs, you can understand our legitimate and unavoidable impatience.

King's open letter asserts nonviolent direct action against unjust laws as a moral imperative, reminding his readers of St Augustine's words – that an immoral law is no law at all. He denounces quietism in the face of injustice:

> Over the past few years, I have consistently preached that nonviolence demands that the means we use must be as pure as the ends we seek. I have tried to make clear that it is wrong to use immoral means to attain moral ends. But now I must affirm that it is just as wrong, or perhaps even more so, to use moral means to preserve immoral ends.

In December 1927, Ambedkar addressed a large gathering at Mahad on the need to eradicate casteism 'by its roots and the root soil'. Four years earlier, the Bombay Legislative Council had passed a resolution that people from the Depressed Classes should henceforth have free access to all places built and maintained by the government. However, resistance from the oppressor castes continued. At Mahad, for instance, Dalits continued to be denied access to the Chowdar Tank. In March 1927, Ambedkar had led a protest march to the tank where he drank some water in a symbolic assertion of equality. Afterwards, the Dalits of the area were ostracized by the caste-Hindus; some were punished with an economic boycott and revocation of their employment or tenancy rights. Speaking of the significance of the second protest action in December, Ambedkar observed:

> At the outset, let me tell those who oppose us that we did not perish because we would not drink water from this Chowdar Tank. We now want to go to the Tank only to prove that, like others, we are also human beings . . . This Conference has been called to inaugurate an era of equality in this land. Removal of untouchability and inter-castes dinners alone will not put an end to our ills. All departments of services such as courts, military, police and commerce should be thrown open to us . . . Hindu society should be reorganized on two main principles – equality and absence of casteism.[4]

Ambedkar's book *What Congress and Gandhi Have Done to the Untouchables* (1945) rebukes those who would not risk social disturbance in order to defeat caste injustice. People who take the line of least resistance cannot be expected, he says, to support a campaign led by 'an army of workers in the rural parts', or to 'encourage the Depressed Classes to fight for their rights', or help 'in any legal proceedings arising there from'. He further issues this challenge regarding the eradication of untouchability:

> I am convinced that it [the line of least resistance] will be ineffective in the matter of uprooting Untouchability. The silent infiltration of rational ideas among the ignorant mass of caste Hindus cannot, I am sure, work for the elevation of the Depressed Classes. First of all, the caste Hindu like all human beings follows his customary conduct in observing Untouchability towards the Depressed Classes. Ordinarily people do not give up their customary mode of behaviour because somebody is preaching against it. But when that

4 Jaffrelot, Christophe. *Dr Ambedkar and Untouchability: Analysing and Fighting Caste*. Permanent Black, 2006, pp. 46-48.

> customary mode of behaviour has or is believed to have behind it the sanction of religion, mere preaching, if it is not resented and resisted, will be allowed to waft along the wind without creating any effect on the mind. The salvation of the Depressed Classes will come only when the caste Hindu is made to think and is forced to feel that he must alter his ways. For that you must create a crisis by direct action against his customary code of conduct. The crisis will compel him to think and once he begins to think he will be more ready to change than he is otherwise likely to be. The great defect in the policy of least resistance and silent infiltration of rational ideas lies in this that they do not compel thought, for they do not produce crisis. The direct action in respect of Chawdar Tank in Mahad, the Kalaram Temple in Nasik and the Guruwayur Temple in Malabar have done in a few days what million days of preaching by reformers would never have done. I therefore strongly recommend this campaign of direct action for securing civic rights of the Depressed Classes, for adoption by the Anti-Untouchability League. I know the difficulties of this campaign, and from such experience as I have of it, I am convinced that the forces in charge of Law and Order must be on our side, if it is to end in success.[5]

Although, as per Article 17 of the Constitution, untouchability has been legally abolished, it continues in practice socially. Speaking of the conditions in India at the time of independence, Ambedkar lamented that while we had nearly achieved political freedom, in socio-economic terms, we did not know how much longer it might take to achieve true equality. In his address to the last meeting of the Constituent Assembly, on 25 November 1949, Ambedkar said:

5 *Dr Babasaheb Ambedkar: Writings and Speeches*. Vol. 9, p. 136.

> On 26 January 1950, we are going to enter into a life of contradictions. In politics we will have equality and in social and economic life we will have inequality. In politics we will be recognizing the principle of one man one vote and one vote one value. In our social and economic life, we shall, by reason of our social and economic structure, continue to deny the principle of one man one value. How long should we continue to live this life of contradictions? How long shall we continue to deny equality in our social and economic life? If we continue to deny it for long, we will do so only by putting our political democracy in peril. We must remove this contradiction at the earliest possible moment or else those who suffer from inequality will blow the structure of political democracy which this Assembly has so laboriously built up.[6]

I had occasion to quote these ideas in judging a case before me. It concerned the breaking down a physical wall of untouchability in Uthapuram village near Madurai. Here, a 600-metre long and 12-foot-high wall had been erected to separate the area of the upper-caste Vellala community from the Dalit habitation. The Dalits now had to make a detour of two kilometres to enter the streets occupied by caste Hindus in the village. The Tamil Nadu Front for Eradication of Untouchability, who discovered this wall, held protest demonstrations demanding that it be razed. Their report brought not just this wall to the notice of the world but a range of other abusive and exclusionary practices. The Dalits were not permitted to worship in the temple. Every time they built a bridge over the sewage drain in their area, it was demolished. The sewage flowing out of the caste-Hindu areas contaminated their water line. They were not permitted to put up arches or decorate the streets when they had an important function. However, the existence of this wall caught the attention of the national media, in

6 *Constituent Assembly Debates: Official Report*. Book No. V, Lok Sabha Secretariat, New Delhi (1999), 3rd print, p. 979.

addition to bothering the conscience of a number of Indians. The protest movements following its discovery resulted in the breaking of the wall. The Vellalas, infuriated by this, recorded their own protest by leaving the village and choosing another place to stay.

Moreover, Dalits were denied the right to worship Muthalamman, the village deity, and the houses of Dalits who protested were attacked. Between 2008 and 2009, many civil and criminal cases were registered on both sides. To bring the continuing violence to an end, the rural district SP, Asra Garg, took several steps to bring about a truce between the two sections. The cases regarding the acceptance of the peace agreement and the withdrawal of cases against both sides came before me.

In my judgment, I recorded Ambedkar's reasoning for the eradication of untouchability, cited above. Here are some extracts on how a settlement was reached:

> In the light of this historic agreement reached between the groups due to the efforts of the District Administration more particularly the police led by Mr. Asra Garg, IPS, the reliefs claimed in these writ petitions have become almost infructuous . . . It is needless to state that the District Administration will take all steps to ensure peace and to implement the terms of settlement in its letter and spirit, so that the strife between two sections for over two decades will be remembered as a thing of the past and the constitutional spirit of Article 17can be firmly established. The District Administration will also give suitable orders within two weeks from today to implement all the demands agreed to in the agreement dated 20 October 2011. The erecting of a bus shelter and removal of obstruction in the pathway and improvement in drainage system shall be implemented at the earliest. They will also monitor the terms of the agreement between the parties. With reference to the withdrawal of criminal cases pending against both parties, as suggested by the Superintendent of Police, Madurai, early

steps will be taken to recommend to the Government for issuing appropriate orders for withdrawal of various crime numbers after complying with all legal requirements under the provisions of the code of criminal procedure. A decision in this regard shall be taken within eight weeks from the date of receipt of copy of this order and the first respondent State shall issue appropriate orders to the District Administration to withdraw those cases.

The Superintendent of Police, Madurai District shall continue to monitor the happenings in the village and to take appropriate corrective action. He shall be responsible in implementing the agreement reached between the two groups, which was filed before this court and accepted as part of the settlement of issues arose between the two sections of the Uthapuram village.

Though Compensations were provided on the basis of the recommendations made by the report submitted by the committee appointed by the court, the offences committed on the Scheduled Caste people are offences under Section 3 of the SC and ST (Prevention of Atrocities) Act. Rule 12(4) provides for grant of relief as per Annexure I in the schedule. The amount of compensations have been revised by the Central Government by way of Gazette notification, dated 23 December 2011. The said compensation will have to be given in two installments, one before trial and another after conclusion of the trial. In this case, the parties have reached a compromise on the major social issues and have also agreed to withdraw the criminal cases, the District Administration without waiting for completion of any trial shall grant compensation in terms of the offence committed against the Scheduled Caste people as per the enhanced compensation ordered by the Central Government vide its notification dated23 December 2011. The same shall be paid within 12 weeks from the date of receipt of copy of this order. If already any amounts were paid towards compensation pursuant to G.O.Ms.No.920, dated 12.09.2009, the same can be adjusted against balance compensation to be paid. Apart from the recommendations made by the court appointed committee and accepted by the State Government, if there are any other claims made by other members belonging to Scheduled Castes of Uthapuram Village, those claims also should be entertained by the District Collector and appropriate compensation should be paid in terms of the SC and ST (Prevention of Atrocities) Act, 1989.[7]

Concluding my judgment, I observed:

The Uthapuram experience shows that if the will of the people is strong, they can find solutions among themselves even in the absence of a State intervention. Such was the fundamental duty imposed under Article 51-A (e) of the Constitution. Ultimately, Uthapuram's message is very clear.

> It was a case of a Wall (caste) which divided
> but their Will (power) united them.

7 *Murugan & Ors. vs State of Tamil Nadu & Ors*, 2012(2) CTC 561. Judgment available on https://indiankanoon.org/doc/137803428/ .

15. THE RIGHT TO WORSHIP IN TEMPLES

Today, we are about to enter the temple. But the entry in the temple would not solve the whole problem. Our problem is comprehensive. It is political, social, religious, economic, educational etc. The issue of Kala Ram Temple entry is an appeal to the Hindu mind. The high caste Hindus deprived us from the far ages. Whether the same Hindus are willing to grant our humanitarian rights will be the question raised from this temple entry satyagraha. Whether the Hindu mind is willing to accept us as human beings, this is the question to be tested through this Satyagraha. The high caste Hindus looked down upon us and treated us even worse than cats and dogs. We wish to know whether those very Hindus would give us the status of man or not. This Satyagraha will provide answer to this question. This Satyagraha is one of the efforts for bringing about a change of heart among the high caste hindus. Hence the success of this effort depends on the Hindu mind-set.[1]

On 2 March 1930, ten days before Gandhi left for Dandi on his salt satyagraha, Ambedkar had launched a temple-entry satyagraha in Nashik. Yet, five years later, he made a decidedly contrasting declaration at the Yeola Conference (1935). At his instance, a resolution was passed opposing participation in satyagrahas. In his speech before 10,000 participants, Ambedkar regretted the years lost in the Kala Ram temple-entry satyagraha, and in the futile quest for acceptance within a religious and social order predicated upon caste. The disabilities and indignities suffered by the Dalits resulted from their being part of the Hindu community. While he

1 *Dr Babasaheb Ambedkar: Writings and Speeches*, Vol. 17 (1982), p. 181.

could not alter the fact that he was born a Hindu untouchable, 'I solemnly assure you,' he added, 'that I will not die a Hindu.'

Much water had run under the bridge between the Dandi March and the Yeola Declaration. The Gandhi-Irwin Pact of March 1931 saw Gandhi released from jail after suspending the Civil Disobedience Movement and agreeing to attend the Second Round Table Conference in London later the same year. In Bombay, to attend a meeting of the Congress Working Committee, he expressed a wish to meet and speak with Ambedkar. On 14 August 1931, the meeting took place at Mani Bhavan, Bombay. This was the first time they had met. Dhananjay Keer, whose biography of Ambedkar appeared in 1954 – within Ambedkar's lifetime – reports their conversation thus:

> GANDHI: Well, Doctor, what have you to say in the matter?
>
> AMBEDKAR: You called me to hear your views. Please tell me what you have to say. Or you may please ask me some questions and I shall answer.
>
> GANDHI: I understand that you have got some grievances against me and the Congress. I may tell you that I have been thinking over the problem of Untouchables ever since my school days – when you were not even born. You may perhaps be knowing what enormous amount of efforts I had put in to incorporate this problem in the programme of the Congress and make it a plank of the Congress platform. The Congress leaders opposed it on the plea that it was a religious and social question and as such it should not be mixed with political ones. This is not all. The Congress has spent not less than rupees twenty lakhs on the uplift of the Untouchables. And it is really surprising that men like you should offer opposition to me and to the Congress. If you have to say anything to justify your stand, you are free to do so.
>
> AMBEDKAR: It is true, Mahatmaji, that you started to think

about the problem of Untouchables before I was born. All old and elderly persons always like to emphasize the point of age. It is also true that because of you the Congress Party gave recognition to the problem. But let me tell you frankly that Congress did nothing beyond giving formal recognition to this problem. You say the Congress spent more than rupees twenty lakhs on the uplift of the Untouchables. I say it was all waste. With such a backing I could have effected an astounding change in the outlook and economic conditions of my people. And in that event it would have been imperative for you to see me long before. But I tell you that the Congress is not sincere about its professions. Had it been sincere, it would have surely made the removal of untouchability a condition, like the wearing of khaddar, for becoming a member of the Congress. No person who did not employ untouchable women or men in his house, or rear up an untouchable student, or take food at home with an untouchable student at least once a week, should have been allowed to be a member of the Congress. Had there been such a condition, you could have avoided the ridiculous sight where the President of the District Congress Committee was seen opposing the temple entry of the Untouchables!

You might say that Congress wanted [lacked] strength, and therefore it was unwise to lay down such a condition. Then my point is that Congress cares more for strength than for principles. This is my charge against you and the Congress. You say the British Government does not show a change of heart. I also say that the Hindus have not shown a change of heart in regard to our problem, and so long as they remain adamant, we would believe neither the Congress nor the Hindus. We believe in self-help and self-respect. We are not prepared to have faith in great leaders and Mahatmas. Let me be brutally frank about it. History tells that Mahatmas, like fleeting phantoms, raise dust, but raise no level. Why should the Congressmen oppose our movement and dub me a traitor?[2]

In 1932, Gandhi went on a fast to put an end to separate electorates for the Depressed Classes –in a major concession, Prime Minister Ramsay MacDonald had recognized the Depressed Classes on par with other religious minorities in India. Gandhi's fast compelled Ambedkar to renounce MacDonald's award of separate electorates and sign the Pune Pact. Gandhi announced that he was going to work henceforth for the right of the oppressed class to enter temples. Recounting the events of this period in his book *What the Congress and Gandhi Have Done to the Untouchables* (1945), Ambedkar wrote:

> To put it briefly, after a short spurt of activity in the direction of removing untouchability by throwing open temples and wells the Hindu mind returned to its original state. The reports appearing in the 'Week to Week' columns of the *Harijan* subsided, became few and far between and ultimately vanished. For myself I was not surprised to find that the Hindu heart was so soon stricken with palsy. For I never believed that there was so much milk of human kindness locked up in the Hindu breast as the 'Week to Week' column in the *Harijan* would have the world believe. As a matter of fact a large part of the news that appeared in the 'Week to Week' was faked and was nothing but a lying propaganda engineered by Congressmen to deceive the world that the Hindus were determined to fight Untouchability.
>
> Few temples if any were really opened and those that were reported to have been opened most of them were dilapidated and deserted temples which were used by none but dogs and donkeys. One of the evil effects of the Congress agitation is

2 Keer, Dhananjay. *Dr Ambedkar: Life and Mission*, Bombay: Popular Prakashan, 1971 (1954), pp. 164–167.

> that it has made the political minded Hindus a lying squad which will not hesitate to tell any lie if it can help the Congress. Thus ended the part which the Hindu public played or was made to appear to play in this Temple-Entry movement. The same fate overtook the Guruvayur Temple satyagraha and the legislation for securing Temple-Entry for the Untouchables.[3]

Already in 1930, speaking to the volunteers assembled at Nashik for the Kala Ram temple-entry movement, Dr Ambedkar had the following to say about Dalits entering the temples:

> Your problems will not be solved by temple entry. Politics, economics, education, religion – all are part of the problem. Today's satyagraha is a challenge to the Hindu mind. Are the Hindus ready to consider us men or not; we will discover this today . . .
>
> We know that the god in the temple is of stone. Darshan and puja will not solve our problems. But we will start out and try to make a change in the minds of the Hindus.[4]

Asked for advice in 1934 regarding the continuation of the movement, he observed that entering temples would not be the final solution to the problems of Dalits:

> I did not launch the temple entry movement because I wanted the Depressed Class to become worshippers of idols which they were prevented from worshipping or because I believed that temple entry would make them equal members in and an integral part of the Hindu society. So far as this aspect of the case is concerned, I would advise the Depressed Class to insist

3 *Dr Babasaheb Ambedkar: Writings and Speeches*, Vol. 9, Govt. of Maharashtra (1982), pp. 114–5.

4 Jaffrelot, Christophe. *Dr. Ambedkar and Untouchability*, Orient Longman Pvt. Ltd, 2005, pp. 50–51

upon a complete overhauling of Hindu society and Hindu theology before they consent to become an integral part of Hindu Society. I started temple entry Satyagraha only because I felt that was the best way of energizing the Depressed Class and making them conscious of their position. As I believe I have achieved that therefore I have no more use for temple entry. I want the Depressed Class to concentrate their energy and resources on politics and education, and I hope that they will realize the importance of both.[5]

However, outside the Ambedkarite sphere, the temple-entry issue would stay on the agenda of communitarian politics. In 1937, the Congress party assumed governance of the Madras Presidency. C. Rajagopalachari (1878–1972) became the first Indian to hold the office of premier, or chief minister of the presidency. Under A. Vaidyanatha Iyer (1890–1955) and N.M.R. Subbaraman (1905–1983) – Congress leaders both – a conference took place on 13 June 1939, to push for 'Harijan' right of entry at the Meenakshi temple of Madurai.

A Tamil publication commemorating A. Vaidyanatha Iyer's birth centenary in 1990 recounted his words:

In Tamil Nadu, Madurai has achieved a special place in the Independence Movement. It has a unique place in effecting Gandhiji's plans. Now, we must also achieve the Harijans entering the Meenakshi temple. I beg the Madurai people to make this happen. I believe that the Madurai people will accept my request . . .

On 8 July 1939, the Harijan entry in the Meenakshi temple took place. Harijans, including P. Kakkan, and a few nadars, a newspaper reporter, and the Tamil Nadu Harijan Seva Sangh's secretary L. N. Gopalswami, started from Iyer's residence at 10

5 Ibid.

AM and were welcomed by the temple Executive Officer R.S. Naidu. After praying to Vinayaka and obtaining his permission, they proceeded to the sanctum of the Goddess Meenakshi and received the prasadam from the priest. From there they went to Lord Chockalinga's sanctum and worshipped there. Then they came out of the temple and informed the gathering that the Harijans' entering the Meenakshi temple had been successfully completed . . .

Supported by the vaideeka (orthodox) leaders Natesa Iyer and Venkatrama Iyer, the following morning the temple priests did not open the temple. They locked the temple up and took away the keys. When the executive officer came to know of this, he informed Iyer. The Government was also informed. Iyer spent a lot of money and engaged several Siva temple priests from different places. Since the temple remained closed till the evening, thousands of devotees had gathered in front of the sannadhi.[6] Four priests brought by Iyer broke open the temple doors and performed rituals that had been stopped from the morning and also conducted the pooja for the evening. The temple's pooja and other rituals were conducted without further complications . . .

The vaideekas too were not inactive. They registered civil and criminal cases against Iyer, Gopalswami, and the Harijans for breaking the tradition of the temple and entering it. Summons were issued to these parties by the Court. But the Court was informed that the Collector was camping in Kodaikanal and would arrive at the Court in the afternoon bringing the Ordinance of the Government to stall civil and criminal actions against these parties. When the hearing started in the afternoon, the Collector presented the Government Order. So the case was permanently set aside. The vaideekas were infuriated. There was widespread talk that they were

6 The forecourt of a temple.

> resorting to black magic to get back at Iyer. After the Madurai temple was opened, temples at AlagarKovil and Palani also opened their doors to the Dalits. It was decided to conduct conferences to open the temples at Srirangam (Ranganatha) and Srivilliputtur (Andal) . . .[7]

After the temple entry at Madurai, C. Rajagoplachari introduced a legislation for the removal of civil and social disabilities from the Depressed Classes. This legislation included the Temple Entry Authorization and Indemnity Act, 1939. The Madras Temple Entry Ordinance 1 of 1939 was promulgated on 17 July 1939. It allowed all Hindus, irrespective of their castes, to worship at temples. All political parties supported this law. It was a victory for Rajaji.

P. Kakkan (1908–1981), who accompanied Vaidyanatha Iyer in entering the Meenakshi temple, faced problems later. In a short booklet on the Dalit leader and three-term member of parliament from the Congress party, Lakshmanan Ilayaperumal (1924–2005), D. Ravikumar writes:

> Kakkan was brought up by Vaidyanatha Iyer who was a Congressman. He was a warden at the Seva Sangh. There was an objection to his wearing footwear and donning a top piece. It was the backward class people who objected. We should not forget that [these objectors] the Kallars[8] were supported by the brahmins. Kakkan did not want any violence. He was Sahajananda's[9] friend and asked him for a letter of

7 *Life History of late A. Vaidyanatha Iyer*, Centenary Souvenir (Tamil) 1990. My translation.

8 A backward caste that is a dominant landowning group in Tamil Nadu. Together with the Agamudaiyars and Maravars, the Kallars make up the Thevar caste formation.

9 Sahajananda (1890–1959), a Dalit spiritual leader and member of the Congress party, was part of the legislative council for Madras from 1926 to 1932 and again from 1936 to 1947. After independence, he was elected to the Tamil Nadu legislative assembly in 1952 and 1957. In 1916, he had

> recommendation. Kakkan's father was a priest. The Kallars wanted him to be removed. Kakkan was then a Member of Parliament. When Sahajananda asked Kakkan how could he give him a letter of recommendation, Kakkan replied that only Sahajananda has influence with Bhakthavatsalam[10] and it was enough if he spoke to Bhakthavatsalam. Sahajananda gave him the letter of recommendation . . .
>
> The Kallars slapped Kakkan's father, the poojari of the Kali temple at Tumbapatti. It was common for the oppressed class people to be poojaris in certain places in Madurai District. Upper caste Hindus stood humbly before them and received vibudi (sacred ash) from them. This is a practice that continues even today.[11]

For all this history, the Dalits are still not given equal rights in the temples of Tamil Nadu. For instance, the right to pull the chariot cords on the outer mada streets[12] around the temples is denied to them. An example of this is the incident at the Kandadevi Swarnamoortheeswarar Temple – around 15 km from Karaikudi in the Sivaganga district. When the Dalits were prevented from pulling the chariot cord, Dr K. Krishnasamy, the President of Puthiya Tamizhagam (New Tamil Nadu] Party, approached the High Court. The division bench headed by Chief Justice Markandeya Katju heard the case and passed a judgment in 2005 saying that pulling the chariot cord was a right of the Dalit, and the Dalits had every right to worship at the temple. The judges ordered

established a mutt and school at Chidambaram, in memory of Nandanar, the medieval Saivite saint and Dalit.

10 Minjur Bhakthavatsalam (1897–1987), a member of the Congress party and chief minister of Madras State from 1963 to 1967, incidentally the last Congress chief minister of Tamil Nadu.

11 Ravikumar, L. *Ilayaperumal Vazhvum Paniyum* (Tamil), Manarkeni Publications, 2010. My translation.

12 The streets surrounding a temple, where the houses of the better-off upper castes are traditionally located.

that severe action be taken against the people who denied the Dalits these rights, and the full responsibility for this lay with the district collector. The following are extracts from the judgment:

> This Court will no longer tolerate such kinds of treatment of the SC/ST Communities as they also are equal citizens of our country and are hence entitled to a life of dignity in view of Article 21 of the Constitution of India, as interpreted by the Supreme Court of India. In our opinion, to deny them the right to participate in the pulling of the Temple Car is a violation of Article 21 of the Constitution, apart from being violative of the orders of the court dated 6.7.1998 and of the Commissioner dated 26.6.1999, and it will simply not be tolerated by this Court . . .
>
> Oppression, atrocities, and humiliation of the Scheduled Castes and Scheduled Tribes is a shameful chapter in our country's history. For thousands of years the Scheduled Castes and Scheduled Tribes in our country have been humiliated and looked down upon. In fact, even today the so-called upper castes and even OBCs often look down upon and insult the members of the Scheduled Castes and Scheduled Tribes. This can no longer be tolerated in this modern age of democracy. Equality is one of the basic features which characterizes this era. Today no people and no community will tolerate being treated as inferior and will oppose such ill-treatment, and will be justified in doing so. The truth is that even today, in many parts of our country Scheduled Castes and Scheduled Tribes are oppressed and humiliated and violence is committed on them . . .
>
> It is alleged that some representatives of the nattar[13] community claim that there is a custom that members

13 Caste leader. Here 18 villages of the Thevar community had their own nattars.

> belonging to the Scheduled Caste and Scheduled Tribe Communities have no right to pull the temple car. Although this contention is denied, yet even assuming that there is such a custom, it will be wholly illegal and unconstitutional, as it is against the right to a life of dignity envisaged in Article 21 of the Constitution. After the promulgation of the Constitution, all customs which are in violation of Articles 14, 21 and other constitutional provisions are null and void, and have to be disregarded, since the Constitution is a fundamental law of the land.
>
> We make it clear that the District Collector cum District Magistrate will be personally held responsible if the order we are passing today is not complied with. The District Collector cum District Magistrate must act fairly to all castes and communities and ensure that everyone is given equal respect in this Car Festival and even otherwise. The District Collector cum District Magistrate will submit a report to this Court about the conducting of the Car Festival and as to whether our orders have been complied with in letter and spirit. This Court will continue monitoring the matter even in future.[14]

Even after this order was passed in 2005, the Kandadevi Nattars ignored it with the support of a local politician who was a minister in the AIADMK government. The Dalits who came from other places to Kandadevi to participate in the chariot procession were stopped at the entrance of Kandadevi with the help of the police. The local Dalits were not allowed to touch the chariot cord. Four Dalits were photographed as if they were touching the cord. With this token gesture made, the Nattar community proceeded to conduct the chariot procession. This atrocity was reported to the High Court, and a contempt petition was filed for action against

14 Puthiya Tamilagam rep. By its President, *Dr. K. Krishnasamy vs State of Tamil Nadu and Ors.*, 2005 (3) *Law Weekly* 140.

the indifference of the district administration. But the judges refused to hear the petition. There is no dearth of revolutionary proclamations followed by cowardly inaction in our country.

L. Ilayaperumal registered his opinion on the justices who refused to hear the case:

> Krishnasamy did not demand the Kandadevi Temple Chariot cord, but the right to pull the cord. Even Christians worshipped there offering Pongal to the deity. Demanding the cord and the right to pull the cord are two different things. It is said that Krishnasamy made the mistake of failing to understand this difference. This is clearly wrong. In reality, it is the judges who committed the mistake. Kandadevi is a small town. It will not take even half an hour for the chariot to go round the town. The judges did not know this and said that the chariot procession should be completed in one hour's time. The chariot procession should be conducted in Kandadevi and the Dalits should have equal rights to pull the chariot cord.[15]

A similar case regarding a temple festival came to me in 2008. Thoppunayagam is a small village near Vattathikottai village in Orathanadu taluk in Thanjavur district. In this village, a law-and-order situation arose in connection with the participation of the Dalits and the other Hindu castes in the temple festival. The tahsildar stopped the festival itself. A case was filed against the tahsildar's action. I dismissed the case and, in my order, observed the following:

> [T]his Court is pained to record that situations like the present one continue even after the dawn of 21st century. Even at the time of worshiping a God, groups are divided on caste lines.

15 Ravikumar, L. *Ilayaperumal Vazhvum Paniyum* (Tamil), Manarkeni Publications, 2010, p. 45. See also Ravikumar's obituary for Ilayaperumal here: https://www.countercurrents.org/dalit-ravikumar300905.htm .

> The dominant community in the village is not willing to accommodate the dalit brethren of the same village even at the altar of the God.[16]

I also pointed out:

> We go against the saying let's unite and pull the chariot together
> And say let's push our brethren
> To the edge of the village
> These people are indeed strange!

Yet another case came to me in 2009 regarding a chariot procession: the trustees of the Mariamman temple had refused to take the deity's chariot through the Dalit colony during the Aadi festival. This happened in Poottai village in Sankarapuram taluk of Villupuram district. When the Kallalurichi tahsildar stopped the festival, stating that it would lead to a law-and-order situation, the temple administration approached the Court in opposition to the tahsildar's order. I dismissed the temple administration's petition and ordered that the district administration ensure the procession of the chariot run through the Dalit colony:

> [T]here is no scope for the Trustees to assert a right of taking the temple car through a particular route thereby denying the right of the Dalits to worship the deity in their colony . . .
>
> [T]he attempt by the Trustees to prevent the Dalits from taking the temple car to their colony during the Temple Car festival held during the month of Aadi cannot be accepted by this Court. Any such order in their favour will amount to perpetuating untouchability which has been specifically prohibited by Article 17 of the Constitution of India. The temple Trustees have failed to establish any custom or usage

16 *S. Rajendran vs Sub Divisional Magistrate, Thanjavur & Ors.*, W.P.(MD) No. 7205 of 2008 dated 7.8.2008.

in charting the route for the deity to be taken in the temple car. For the last three years, due to their intransigence and caste supremacy, the festival has been stopped. It is not as if there is no place in the colony by which the deity can reach the Dalit, but there is [need for some] place in the heart of the caste Hindus of the village to accept the Dalits as their brethren so as to have a whole community worship [together]. In such circumstances, the Government cannot be a spectator in denying the rights of the Dalits of the colony and the constitutional mandate will have to be enforced through all legal means.[17]

17 *C. Arumugam & Ors. vs The Revenue Divisional Officers-cum Magistrate &Ors.*, 2010 (4) MLJ (Mad) 1077.

16. THE BASIC CIVIL RIGHTS OF THE DALITS

Mahatma Gandhi said India lives in her villages. In reality, every village contains two villages. The people of the four varnas live in the main village and the *panchamas* in a colony away from the village. The term colony is an apt name for the Dalits' locality, for they are held in servitude to the needs of the villagers, the same way that empires kept their colonies to be exploited for selfish benefit. Ambedkar's excoriation of India's villages is as well-known as Gandhi's fond view of them. On 4 November 1948, during the debates of the Constituent Assembly, Ambedkar took on those who wished India's new Constitution to reflect an imaginary past of ancient village republics:

> Another criticism against the Draft Constitution is that no part of it represents the ancient polity of India . . . The love of intellectual Indians for the village community is of course infinite if not pathetic (laughter) . . . No doubt the village communities have lasted where nothing else lasts. But those who take pride in the village communities do not care to consider what little part they have played in the affairs and the destiny of the country; and why? . . . mere survival has no value. The question is on what plane they have survived. Surely on a low, on a selfish level . . . I am therefore surprised that those who condemn provincialism and communalism should come forward as champions of the village. What is the village but a sink of localism, a den of ignorance, narrow-mindedness and communalism? I am glad that the Draft Constitution has

discarded the village and adopted the individual as its unit.[1]

In the same debate, Ambedkar also noted the sober truth that 'democracy in India is only the top-dressing on an Indian soil that is essentially undemocratic.' His unease about the new Constitution embarking on a 'life of contradictions' has been amply justified in the subsequent decades.

The Dalits are denied even basic civil rights. The government and the police are together in this. Even in villages where untouchability is not explicit, it cannot be said to have been eradicated. Atrocities like Dalits being flogged or forced to consume a solution made of dung may no longer be commonplace. Still, other forms of untouchability continue to exist, such as separate cremation/burial grounds, separate roads, separate access to water bodies, separate cups in tea shops, the job of removing garbage, of the dead, of beating *parai* drums, the denial of temple entry and arbitrary prohibitions on riding cycles and using footwear.

Even today, there are no connecting roads from the Dalit colonies to the main roads in many villages. There are no lands available to Dalits to build houses. They have separate cremation/burial grounds, and there are no roads leading to them. News media recently revealed that a Dalit's dead body had to be carried through cane fields in Villupuram district. Only after this revelation the district collector visit the village and promise the Dalits that a road would be built to their burial ground.

In 1992, in Aandakudi village near Thiruvaiyaaru, the dominant castes tried to prevent the dead body of a Dalit from being taken through their streets. Later, they filed a civil suit in the district munsif court, Thiruvaiyaaru, to permanently prevent the dead bodies of Dalits from being carried through their streets and

1 4 November 1948, Constituent Assembly Debates. Available on http://164.100.47.194/Loksabha/Debates/Result_Nw_15.aspx?dbsl=144&ser=&smode= .

even obtained a stay order. Challenging this on behalf of the Dalits, V. Rajendran filed a suit under Article 227 of the Constitution in the Madras High Court, making use of its special supervisory powers.

The Madras High Court heard the case and observed that the suit filed by the dominant castes in the District Civil Court was not maintainable as it perpetuated untouchability prohibited by Article 17 of the Constitution. The Court further pointed out that filing such suits is prohibited under Section 13 of the Protection of Civil Rights Act, 1955. It ordered that the complaint of the dominant castes be struck off from the Court's Register and this order be sent to all the civil courts through a circular. The following is S.S. Subramani's final order passed in this case in 1996:

> By Section 17 of the Protection of Civil Rights Act, 1955, the custom or practice pleaded in the plaint stands abrogated, and Section 13 of the said Act prohibits the Court from entertaining any suit of continuing the suit or to pass a decree, or even refuse to execute the decree, if it is against the provisions of the Act. Even though the word used is 'entertain' taking into consideration the context in which it is used, it follows that the Court is prohibited from taking into consideration the plaint in any manner. Before issuing summons, the Court has to apply its mind, whether such a suit could be entertained, and whether there is any statutory bar [to doing so]. In this case, even though the State has been impleaded, no Section 80 C.P.C., notice has been issued, and permission has also been sought for dispensing with Section 80 C.P.C. notice, it is thereafter the suit ought to have been registered. At least at that time, the Court should have applied its mind, whether the proposed suit could be entertained in a Court of law. . .
>
> Learned counsel for the petitioner is justified in invoking the provisions of Article 227 of the Constitution of India in

> filing this Revision. When Subordinate Courts act irrationally while taking cognizance of suits, the consequence of which will be severe on the community at large, this Court has a duty to see that the subordinate judiciary acts within its limits. It should also see that the Subordinate Courts act in accordance with the law. . .
>
> But, according to me, that is not exhaustive when we look into the provisions of the Protection of Civil Rights Act, 1955. When the Act says that the Court shall not continue the suit and also uses the word 'entertain', according to me, a little more strict meaning will have to be applied. Even at the very threshold, the plaint will have to be taken off the file.[2]

In 1978, the Government of Tamil Nadu passed a Special Act to acquire lands to distribute plots to Dalits and build cremation/burial grounds and roads leading to them. In 1981, a division bench of the Madras High Court struck down the law as unconstitutional. The case was taken to the Supreme Court, which decided in 1995 that the law was not violative of the Constitution.[3]

Even after that, hundreds of suits were filed in the Madras High Court. In these suits, it was argued that the district collector had not followed proper procedure. In the years 2007 and 2008, as a judge in the Madras High Court, I dismissed hundreds of writ petitions regarding the acquisition of land for the benefit of the Dalits. This removed the impediments to several beneficial schemes for the Dalits launched between 1978 and 2008.

In one such case, a former Advocate General and a Senior Advocate appeared. I told him that I was pained by his appearance in such a case. I asked him how, after having been Advocate General

2 *V. Rajendran vs The District Munsif, Thiruvaiyaru & Ors*, 1996(2) *Law Weekly* 435. Judgment available on https://www.legitquest.com/case/v-rajendran-v-the-district-munsif-thiruvaiyaru-others/6C2C1 .

3 *State of Tamil Nadu vs Anandiammal*, 1995 (1) SCC 519. Judgment available on https://indiankanoon.org/doc/1159928/ .

for ten years, he could not understand the atrocities perpetrated on Dalits. I also told him that no mere law for acquiring lands for the Dalits would be enough. What was needed was a place for them in his heart.

He shocked me by replying that atrocities on the Dalits were a thing of the past. I dismissed his case. Still, I was not satisfied. I visited the Landmark bookshop that evening and bought *Dalits in Dravidian Land*, a collection of articles by the journalist S. Viswanathan published in the magazine *Frontline*, on anti-Dalit atrocities between 1995 and 2004. I sent it to the senior advocate with the following note:

> Dear Sir,
> In connection with the opinions you expressed in the Court this morning, I am sending a book. Please make sure you read it. Afterwards we shall continue our debate on the conditions of Dalits in Tamil Nadu.
> With regards,
> Chandru

The senior advocate called me the same night and expressed regret for what he had said in court. He said that the book threw light on the continuing atrocities on the Dalits in Tamil Nadu.

The Government of Tamil Nadu tried to acquire 49 cents[4] of land in Usilampatti, Madurai district, for the use of Dalits. The owner of the land had been waging a legal battle against the government since 1980. He approached the court several times and managed to obtain a stay against the acquisition of the land. When the case came before me in 2008, I dismissed his petition and ordered that the land be acquired immediately, and in addition, a fine of Rs 10,000 be levied on the landowner. The following is an extract from the case:

4 A hundred cents make an acre.

> [T]he correspondence including the legal notice issued by the petitioner clearly shows that he was not in any mood to part with the property even though vesting of the lands had already taken place and the lands vest with the State Government. It is clear that by a brute force brought in by the petitioner, he is able to declare that he is still cultivating land and he is in possession . . . Such kind of naked defiance by an individual against the legal proceedings taken by the State cannot be countenanced.
>
> The last argument, that public purpose was not achieved, is clearly mischievous because it is the petitioner who is holding on to the land for the last 30 years, despite there being an acquisition under a valid legislation to provide land for the Harijan Welfare Scheme. In the present case, the notification was issued for the purpose of providing house sites to the Harijans of Goundanpatty village and the petitioner cannot be allowed to thwart a social welfare scheme by continuously raiding this Court with a series of writ petitions. It is rather saddening to note that the Dalits of the village were unable to get house site even 30 years after a valid notification was made. It also shows the lethargy on the part of the state in taking quick steps to implement the scheme for which the acquisition was made . . .
>
> The first and second respondents are hereby directed to take over the land and proceed to implement the Scheme for which it is originally acquired within four weeks and also report compliance to this Court.[5]

In the same way, in 1998, under the new law, the Villupuram district collector ordered the acquisition of land to distribute plots among Dalits and build connecting roads from the colony to the main road in Kadapperi Kuppam village in Vanur taluk. The owner

5 *P. Ponniah vs The District Collector, Madurai & Ors.*, W.P.(MD) No.9654 of 2005 dated 16.9.2008.

of the land filed a writ petition, which came before me ten years later. I dismissed the petition making the following observation:

> Before it is concluded, it must be noted that the constitutional validity of T. N. Act 31 of 1978 was upheld by the Supreme Court in the year 1995 and a Full Bench of this Court has settled the controversy on the modalities of the procedure involved in the Land Acquisition for Harijan Welfare Schemes in the year 2006. It is a pity that these cases which are filed one decade before have virtually frustrated the welfare scheme conceived for the welfare of Dalits. Thirty years have gone by and the law conceived for the Dalits remains a paper proposition.
>
> A number of anti-discrimination statutes and positive-benefit provisions exist in Indian law for the protection and benefit of Dalits, tribals, and other backward classes of society. But the implementation and enforcement of these laws is poor. Dalits face social, linguistic and systematic barriers that become virtually impossible to overcome in the face of an often hostile system and an insensitive civil administration. The entire system is designed to exclude and ostracize Dalits.[6]

However, Dalits who converted to Christianity still had travails. In the religion they embraced, they were not given equal rights, and they continued to be untouchables among Hindus. We have already seen that the Christian Dalits continue to live in separate colonies. Thus, the atrocity of untouchability continues, and on top of that, they are denied the concessions given to Hindu Dalits.

In 1985, Soosai, a cobbler in Chennai, filed a case in the Supreme Court challenging a concession given to Dalits on the basis of religion. An Adi Dravidar convert to Christianity, Soosai

6 *G. LakshiAmmal & Another vs The District Collector, Villupuram & Ors.*, W.P.No. 15454 of 1999 dated 3/12/2008. Judgment available on https://indiankanoon.org/doc/136061/?type=print .

had applied for the allotment of a 'bunk' – being distributed free at the time as welfare assistance to cobblers who worked by the roadside. However, under the law, his application had been rejected since, as it then stood, only Hindu Dalits – along with some Sikh groups within Punjab (the Kabirpanthis, Ravidasias, Sikligars, and Mazhabis) – qualified as Scheduled Castes. Chief Justice P.N. Bhagwati heard Soosai's petition and dismissed it, observing that it was unacceptable to say that atrocities against Dalits continued even after conversion and that there was little evidence to show that they continued to be considered untouchables. He observed:

> It is apparent that for the purpose of the Constitution the constitutional provisions relating to Scheduled Castes are intended to be applied to only those members of the castes enumerated in the Constitution (Scheduled Castes) Order, 1950 who profess the Hindu or the Sikh religion. Clearly, if it can be contemplated that a Christian belongs to one of those castes, he is barred by reason of paragraph 3, from being regarded as a member of a Scheduled Caste and is, therefore, not entitled to the benefit of the constitutional provisions relating to Scheduled Castes.[7]

In 1996, Supreme Court Justice K. Ramaswamy heard a case about issuing a community certificate to a Scheduled Caste person who had converted to Christianity. He recorded in his judgment how atrocities continue on the Scheduled Castes in South India even after conversion, mentioning the case of Valsamma Paul. Valsamma, a forward class (Syrian) Christian, had married a Latin Catholic fisherman and joined her husband's church and community – losing her former social status. However, when she was awarded a position at Cochin University as a Catholic, the appointment came to be challenged on the grounds of her birth.

7 *Soosai vs Union of India & Ors.*, 1985 (Supp) SCC 590. Judgment available on https://indiankanoon.org/doc/1724190/ .

The Supreme Court had decided against her. Justice Ramaswamy observed:

> In South India, if a person converts from Hindu religion to another religion, the original caste, without violating the tenants of the new order to which he has gone, as a matter of common practice continues to exist from times immemorial. If a person abjures his old religion and converts to a new one, there is no loss of caste.[8]

After the dismissal of Soosai's petition, the Catholic Bishops Council had met Prime Minister P.V. Narasimha Rao and requested that discrimination based on religion be removed through an amendment to the law. In 1996, the Congress government placed the amendment before the parliament but did not make a whole-hearted attempt to pass it. The Congress government's bill, which was awaiting BJP's support, lapsed once the parliament session came to an end.

Again, in 2004, a case was filed in the Supreme Court against the uneven grant of concessions to Dalits, which amounted to discrimination on the basis of religion. The matter is still pending. In 2011, a three-judge sitting heard the case and ordered that the details of the suit be published on the government's website for consideration by the public and that the opinions of the Commission for the Scheduled Caste and Scheduled Tribe be obtained.

In the midst of these confusions, in 2012, when a Dalit convert to Christianity died in a village in Tamil Nadu, the caste-Hindus prevented his body from being buried in the village's common burial ground. They were adamant in their stand that even though he was converted, he should be buried in the separate burial ground

8 *Valsamma Paul (Mrs) vs Cochin University & Ors.*, 1996 (3) SCC 545. Judgment available on https://indiankanoon.org/doc/4735043/ .

for the Dalits. In the face of strong opposition and intervention by the revenue officials, the body was buried in the common burial ground. The Dalit Christians of that village still live in fear of repercussions.

The atrocities against the Scheduled Castes, whether Hindus or converts to other religions are the same. Under the Scheduled Castes and Scheduled Tribes (Prevention of Atrocities) Act, calling a Dalit by his caste name is a crime, but if s/he is a Christian, this law does not apply and it will not be considered a crime.

In Thamanur village in the Senji taluk of Villupuram district, 37 Adi Dravidar families had converted to Christianity. To distribute plots to them under the new law in Tamil Nadu (Tamil Nadu Acquisition of Land for Harijan Welfare Scheme Act 1978), the district collector issued an order for land acquisition. The families qualified as homeless, and the total acquisition amounted to a mere 0.87 hectares of dry land. However, in his order of 1998, the collector had mentioned that the land was being acquired for the Adi Dravidar Christians of Thamanur village. Making use of this mistake, the owner of the land filed a writ petition in the High Court. It was argued that under the new law, land could be acquired only for Hindu Adi Dravidars and that Adi Dravidar converts to Christianity could not be considered Scheduled Caste. Meanwhile, the revenue officials granted pattas to the 37 families. Since the case was pending in the court, they could not use the lands given to them. This case came to me for hearing ten years after the collector's order was challenged. The original petitioner was dead, and two of his descendants pursued the challenge. The argument of the landowner was legally tenable. If I accepted it and cancelled the order for acquiring the land, 37 Dalit families would lose their allotment. Under the Land Acquisition Act of 1984, there was no objection to lands being acquired for a public purpose. The landowner did not obey the order that he compromise with the collector and sell the lands at market value. So, in my order, I said the following and gave directions to the district collector:[9]

> The Tamil Nadu Act 31 of 1978 is intended to acquire land only for Harijan Welfare Schemes and the definition of Harijan is as listed in the Presidential notification issued under Article 341 of the Constitution. The Christian Adi Dravidars stood excluded from the list of castes contained in the Presidential notification. The exclusion of Christian Adi Dravidars from the list of Scheduled Castes was also held to be not unconstitutional by the Supreme Court in Soosai's case (cited *supra*). But it must be pointed out that the very issue has again been taken up and is being heard by a larger bench of the Supreme Court. It is yet to decide the validity or otherwise of the exclusion of the Christian convert Adi Dravidars from availing the benefits provided under Article 46 of the Constitution.
>
> Since the respondents wanted to utilize the land to provide house sites to Adi Dravidar people of the village who are converts to Christianity, this Court suggested to the learned counsel for the petitioner to find out whether his client was inclined to negotiate with the district collector to settle the compensation issue since the land has been used for a public purpose though not prescribed under the State Act. He was also informed that even if the acquisition under the State Act has been nullified, still the State can resort to acquisition under the Central Act 1 of 1894 since the bona fides of the public purpose is not disputed. But after instructions from his client, the learned counsel for the petitioner informed this Court that his client is not willing to settle the matter through any private negotiation.
>
> This Court is not inclined only to set aside the acquisition made under Tamil Nadu Act 31 of 1978 and leave matters at

9 *Gopal Gounder (deceased) & Ors. vs The Special Tahsildar, Land Acquisition, Adi Dravidar Welfare Scheme, Gingee & Ors.*, 2009 (4)M.L.J 1267 (Mad). Judgment available on https://indiankanoon.org/doc/787075/ .

that. It is just and necessary to give further directions to the second respondent District Collector and the third respondent State of Tamil Nadu. While the acquisition under the Tamil Nadu Act 31 of 1978 will stand set aside, this will not preclude the respondents from resorting to the acquisition under the Central Act 1 of 1894 for providing house sites to Christian Adi Dravidars of the Thamanur village by taking appropriate steps for issuing a proper notification and proceed to acquire the lands for the purpose of distributing them to the 37 beneficiaries already identified by the respondents.

The respondents, if so desired, shall take steps to issue notification within a period of twelve weeks from the date of receipt of a copy of this order. Till such time, status quo regarding possession of the land will continue.